STUDIES
IN
MODERN
PHILOLOGY

5

STUDIES IN MODERN PHILOLOGY

Series Editors
Károly Mannherz
János Szávai

AKADÉMIAI KIADÓ · BUDAPEST 1988

MODERN
LATIN AMERICAN
FICTION

A return to didacticism

by

Katalin Kulin

AKADÉMIAI KIADÓ, BUDAPEST 1988

Translated by Eszter Molnár

Chapter IV/Mario Vargas Llosa/
translated by Fruzsina Balkay

ISBN 963 05 4686 8

Printed in Hungary
by Akadémiai Kiadó és Nyomda Vállalat Budapest

CONTENTS

INTRODUCTION

Since the turn of the century we have constantly
been forewarned of the impending death of the novel. The
death-knell is stilled whenever the genre is revived in
another country or on another continent; the reader's
heart is set at rest: the crisis was not so terrible
after all. But the writer cannot feign indifference and
bypass the question. The stake is always great, the
crisis real, and the patient truly in need of miraculous
healers. The Latin American authors emerging around the
sixties fortunately proved to be such. But their task was
not an easy one. The well-known precept stating that only
the truly particular can become truly universal is an
excellent formula save that its components vary according
to the given period and the given writer. These Latin
American authors have demonstrated that their inspiration
is of native — indigenous — origin, but were able to
recognize the particular — to reverse the precept — only
by perceiving the universal. It was not always easy to
find examples and forebearers at home — especially not
many who or which could command interest within the
confines of the country or continent. It is quite under-

standable that they turned for guidance to North America and to Europe.

Above all they found themselves drawn towards Faulkner. His provincial towns with their well-to-do families and illiterate poor, overcast by an atmosphere fraught with tension due to social inequality, racial prejudice and cultural disparity were all familiar to them.

Dos Passos aroused their interest chiefly by his original, modern technique, which lent itself particularly well to the presentation of the multifarious metropolis.

They first took possession of Europe through the medium of great authors like the Argentine Jorge Luis Borges, the Guatemalan Miguel Angel Asturias, the Cuban Alejo Carpentier. As a result of their mediation, many authors felt the pressing need of becoming personally acquainted with Europe. There, and especially in Paris, surrealism is once again in vogue and the "nouveau roman" is all the rage. There, they have condemned the old rhotorics and are searching for a new, more suggestive, more instinctive (or more accurate), more authentic means of expression. It is the golden age of language-centered theories of literary criticism. The structuralists seek the literariness, the essence of esthetic quality within the linguistic matter, the text of the work of art. In an impassive, objective manner they are to a certain degree reformulating the notions of the surrealists concerning the magic of the language. The written word is no longer the means of expressing reality — the supposed servant is in fact an almighty wizard, capable of creating a new reality — as Borges' short stories attest. In a wider sense of the word, Faulkner too creates a new language — if any system of communication may be accepted as language. The symbols of his system are mythical motifs — situations and events which are easily translatable to the communications system of peoples differing in mentality and culture, notably to that of the African-origin black population of the USA. The inherited and the borrowed both direct the attention of the Latin American authors to the language, of which they value the following two characteristics above all: as a system of communication it is a vehicle of universal correspondance; as discourse it is the structural model of incidental, discontinuous, fragmentary reality.

However paradoxical it may seem, Latin America's grave social-political situation, fraught with conflicts as it is, encouraged the rebirth of the moribund novel in an unparalleled way. The genre does not readily suffer being deprived of conflicts characteristic of epic works since the beginning of time, and is impoverished if it is not, or is only to a limited extent, based on collective experience (as the French nouveau roman has proved). Though the novels to be discussed are not all as conspicuously historically-socially inspired as those of Rulfo, García Márquez and Vargas Llosa, a social confrontation is their undisclosed precedent (*The Shipyard*) or they study the possibility of breaking down the boundaries between personalities within a community, as in *62. A Model Kit*. This conflict or confrontation demands a plot, gladly welcomed by the reader hungry for a story. At the same time the authors, schooled on cultures sprung from social conditions more highly developed than those of their own country, are not satisfied with the spontaneity of the plot, but encode their highly ideologized concept of the world (pervaded by a

9

specific social attitude or philosophy) within it, in
the arrangement of the components of the story, in the
characteristics of the narration, in the discourse.
This encoded authorial concept of the world, despite
its indirectness, is nevertheless effective in guiding
the reader in a specific direction, which may range from
the recognition of existential problems to a call for
action. In the last analysis we may say that the gulf
between the ideological-artistic attitude of the writers
and the political-economical backwardness of their
countries created an ideal epical situation for Latin
American narrative literature.

In traditional novel-writing the plot, the characters and the environment have a specific place and role.
By changing this place and role the Latin American
writers have assisted the revival of the novel. In
Rulfo's work it is the climate (and by this word we mean
not only weather conditions but also geographic location
and sound-environment); in *The Shipyard* it is the behaviour of the characters (more exactly, the nuances of
difference in behaviour) that set in motion the narrative; and in García Márquez's case the mythical motifs
do not maintain their original attributive role (relating
to characters, situations or atmosphere) but assume a
more active role and function as structural instigators
of the events. The characters, environment and plot of
Conversation in the Cathedral assume the roles customary
for them in realistic novels, but their factual value is
rendered doubtful by Vargas Llosa's discourse, in which
time loses its rationality, or rather the rational becomes irrational. Julio Cortázar changes the generic
function of the characters, the action and the environ-

ment, for *62...* as we shall see, only appears to be a story, it is in reality a meditation.

The change of role thus takes place in every work to be discussed. The reallotment of functions necessarily affects the arrangement of the narration. The structure of the novel wrested from factual time is static or cyclic, either because the author alters the sequence of events (Rulfo), or because several periods are piled one upon the other in an anachronistic order (García Márquez), or because almost identical patterns of behaviour are daubed upon each other to replace the action (Onetti), or because time is made irrational by the contradictory sequence of events (Vargas Llosa), or because any type of sequence is made impossible by a character taking part in several events simultaneously (Cortázar). This last type, despite its animatedness, does not in fact move forward, that is, does not in essence, differ from the static type. A characteristic form of cyclic construction is the vortex (Onetti), the labyrinth (Vargas Llosa) and the simultaneously timeless and labyrinth type (Cortázar).

The static and the cyclic (repeating its endless revolutions, closing in upon itself) type of construction can both characterize only this *a priori* given world, accepted as such from the outset. Both types attest a tragic attitude, for neither promises hope of advancement. There is a curious contradiction between the authors' for the most part rather progressive political beliefs and the pessimism reflected in their methods, even though this pessimism is to a certain extent justified by the continent's social-political conditions.

Besides the rearrangement or change of roles another common feature of the works under discussion is that instead of a direct portrayal of reality, they offer a model of a possible world.

Whatever the author's aim may be, the model he creates in his work is always monitory, *ad absurdum,* and revealing a given social or collective (or not collective) mode of life, arouses a desire in the reader to replace it by a more meaningful mode of existence. The therapeutical function of a work of art is not a new idea, but in these novels the deeply personal injury is collective, communal; every character suffers it from the same "hand". This is the neuralgic point of junction which determines each and every one of them, be it placed primordially in society and only secondarily in the human state of existence or vice versa. Most analyses attempt to prove that the action or injury assuming human form is always Janus-faced. The question — and it is not an easy one — is to determine which face makes the deeper impression, that which strikes the eye immediately, placed as it is on the surface of the narrative, or that which is only revealed through the method — the system that "propels" the narration and prompts questioning and investigation by the void it leaves or by its barely implied features.

However hopeless a world that inspires static or cyclic narrative construction, deriving from barren repetition, may seem, the authors of the works under discussion do not renounce the demand of immanent intelligence. Though they may not aspire to a portrayal of the totality of the world, they see history as a process which has a beginning, an end, and an ordinate central point — immanent truth — since their works are, in one form or another, constructed. In this respect even *62...* is no exception; though its beginning and end are inter-

changeable, the central point — the point of departure
and the goal of the meditation — attests to the inextin-
guishable desire for immanent truth.

x x x

In the succeeding chapters one work by each of the
afore-mentioned authors shall be analysed (Rulfo's novel
shall be discussed in comparison with one of his short
stories). Different modes of approach shall be used in
each case, according as whichever is the most suitable,
in our opinion, for a most effective revelation of the
system actuating the narration, that is, of the author's
method.

This method corresponds to the author's image of the
world. A world image involves much more than the attitude
implied by the author's ideology. A writer grasps the
whole of human existence intellectually and emotionally
alike, and the divined mystery has as much right to be
included in this image as the establishable fact.

Our analyses — excepting that relating to *Conversation in the Cathedral*, which is based entirely upon it —
shall be supplemented by the main characteristics of the
discourse of the given works; thus we shall refer to the
moment eliciting the chain of the narrative, the relation
between the time of the action and that of the narration,
the mode of narration: direct, indirect, summarizing,
and the frequencies caused by repetition. These characteristics in part assist in the establishing of the
similarities and dissimilarities between the works under
discussion, and in part strengthen or, through further
interpretation, enrich the conclusions drawn from our
analyses.

I. JUAN RULFO

The climate

In the oeuvre of every writer there are certain
phenomena, occuring repeatedly, albeit in a slightly
different, or even directly contrary form that merit
special attention. In the short story entitled *Luvina*
and in the novel entitled *Pedro Páramo* the protagonist
approaching the scene of the action from elsewhere, from
"without" is such a concurrence. This approach, in the
literal as in the figurative sense of the word, bears a
double advantage. A stranger's sharper, fresher glance
may discover many things that have become so familiar,
so natural to a local inhabitant that they escape his
notice. At the same time the outsider is aware of his
ignorance and therefore asks questions to gather information, and listens to the tales and recollections of those
familiar with the ways of the region. To the traveller
on his way to Luvina it is a man returned from the
village who relates his experiences; and in the novel
Juan Preciado is told of the events occurring during his
father's lifetime by the village ghosts, that is, by
those who, because they are no longer living, have also
departed from the region in question.

Neither he who approaches nor he who looks back is present at the scene of the action. In *Luvina* neither of them shall be; and Juan Preciado shall live in Comala for a short time only. Soon after he gets there he too will be dead, "departed" like those who advise him.

The protagonist of both works is a traveller, the nameless figure of the short story (be it he who is heading for Luvina or he who is relating his experiences there) like Juan Preciado, Pedro Páramo's son.

One of the most ancient literary subjects of the world is the tale of the hero setting out on a long journey. In fairy tales the poor shepherd boy or the youngest son can win the princess' hand only after long peregrinations, and Ulysses, the prototype of every traveller, could return home only after twenty years of wandering. In fairy tales happiness is promised to lie at the end of the road, but the adventures experienced and trials endured during the journey are almost always directed at the traveller's discovery of the world and/or himself. According to Saint John Chrysostom the Bible considers man a wayfarer, a pilgrim on earth. It is no doubt a coincidence, but an interesting coincidence that the name Saint John appears in both works: Luvina's full name is San Juan de Luvina, and Pedro Páramo's beloved is called Susana San Juan.

The traveller searching for happiness, his country, his home is a wanderer, just like he who roams the earth in vain in search of refuge, a place of rest. Juan Preciado, like the nameless traveller returned from Luvina and he who is on his way there, sets out to find his home. Each of them is driven, lured by a dream.

In those days I was strong. I was full of ideas — you know we're all full of ideas. And one goes with

the idea of making something of them everywhere. (*1*)
I couldn't stop thinking and even dreaming about it,
and building a whole world around that Pedro Páramo.
That's why I came to Comala. (*2*)

The impelling force of the dream is heightened by
the nostalgia which the characters feel for the place,
for the goal of their journey. The man returned from
Luvina reviles the village and the rotten liquor you can
get there, but in the end orders that same drink in the
pub. In Juan Preciado's case it is his mother who planted
the yearning for the beautiful valley of Comala in his
breast, and it is this yearning that compels him to set
out on his quest for his father. Attraction and repulsion
are strangely intermingled in their hearts: such is the
nature of the bitter love they feel for their native
land, for their birth-place.

It is an age-old custom in tales and myths alike to
provide the traveller with an escort on his journey, a
companion to assist him on the road, one who is familiar
with the ways of the strange land. Dante's famed guide
Virgil becomes a simple carter in Rulfo's novel. This
carter will give up his place and role to the traveller
returned from Luvina in the short story, to the village
ghosts in the novel. The journey ends in a similar
fashion in both pieces: the nameless narrator concludes
his tale of Luvina by saying the experiences and ordeals
he had to endure there "wore him out, finished him"; and
in the novel Juan Preciado dies, is killed by his experiences.

Juan Preciado's short life is lengthened as it were
by his father's long, richly adventurous life, the young
traveller's in the short story by the experiences of the
narrator returned from Luvina. Old and young traverse

together the entire walk of life, even though they do
not stand for identical stages separately. They stand
proxy for each other and complement one another not
because their characteristics are similar or contrary
but because they have embarked upon the same venture:
to discover, explore and come to know the world and themselves.

Of the travellers we learn nothing apart from the
trait common to them all: their journey. Though Rulfo
divulges more about his personages in the novel, their
personality — even that of Pedro Páramo, depicted with
extraordinarily forceful strokes — arouses interest only
by its negation, attesting that it cannot mean redemption
from the fate awaiting them all: from the bitterness
caused by unfulfilled dreams.

Another common feature is their ability and determination to pursue the journey to its end, to traverse
the interior and exterior provinces of the unknown realms
of existence. The novel naturally offers more scope for
nuances and thus a certain progressivity can be felt in
the identical tendencies of the various characters.

Even the differences between the two works serve
only to reveal the duality — right and wrong side — of
an identical reality. The short story allows larger
scope to nature than to the inhabitants of the village,
whilst in the novel it is the people who are brought
out in strong relief, even though there are only ghosts
to roam the streets of Comala and there are still people
living in Luvina. The author therefore proceeds in a
manner quite contrary to what can be expected.

Based on this paradox, the author's method estab-
lishes further connections between the two works. He
who is heading for Luvina wishes to become acquainted

with the way of life of those living there. The deserted
streets, the locked doors, the people hiding in their
houses without giving the slightest signs of life, the
women venturing out of their homes garbed in black
dresses and shawls and then only at night, their silence
— all this is a negation of life and points towards
death. The details of their everyday lives we learn only
through negatives. There are no men in the village, there
is nothing to eat — there is nothing. Only nature reveals
details, determines, fashions, arouses the atmosphere of
the place in the reader. The rare natural manifestations
of this barren land, the stones, the stunted plants hurt
and wound. The inhabitants are silent, but the bleak,
desolate country-side cries out and shouts to be heard.
Rulfo connects the lifeless, or at least motionless
objects to nouns, adjectives and verbs that express
injurious, offensive noise, blows, cutting, splitting.
Deep fissures cleave the earth, sad little plants clutch
at the mountain cliffside, and the chicalote

>...scratches the air with its spiky branches, making
>a noise like a knife on whetstone. (3)

The wind

>... scratches like it had nails ... scraping the
>walls, tearing off strips of earth, digging with its
>sharp shovel under the doors... (4)

Rulfo humanizes nature, endowing it with the ability
to suffer and the intention to wound. Plants have hands,
clouds are like inflated bladders, that is, the plants
are like suffering and struggling humans, the clouds
like living beings that come and go as unexpectedly and
as unpredictably as the men of Luvina. The wind has a
tool (a sharp shovel) just as people do.

18

You can see the figure of the wind
... sweeping along Luvina's streets, bearing behind
it a black blanket (5)
and the wires
... twanged with each gust of wind like the gnashing
of teeth. (6)
Objects are humanized and humans are objectified.
The author speaks of the "hinges" of people's bones and
that there
... smiles are unknown as if people's faces had been
frozen. (7)
The old people raise and lower their heads "until
the springs go slack" (8) and the menfolk
... plant another child in the bellies of their
women. (9)
As a consequence of the objectification people become
inert, lifeless, passing by
.. like shadows, hugging the walls of the houses (10)
more dead than alive.

In *Pedro Páramo* there are fewer signs of objectification, but we must not forget that in the novel, with
the exception of Juan Preciado, all the characters are
ethereal, without a body, and so are not people, living
human beings in effect. True to his paradox method Rulfo
portrays them as genuine, veritable beings, and endows
them with human physical characteristics, as he did with
the plants in *Luvina*. Juan Preciado, meeting the first
ghost in Comala, sums up his impressions in this way
I knew that her voice was a living human voice. That
she had teeth in her mouth, and a tongue that moved
when she talked, and eyes like the eyes of everybody
else on earth. (11)

But of himself, the only living human being in Comala, he says

My body seemed to be floating, it was so limp, and you could have played with it as if it were a rag doll. (12)

In the original the allusion is more obvious still. Literally, the sentence means: The strength seemed to leave my body, it became slack and limp, and I fell in a heap like a rag doll. The novel and the short story are related not only by their similar, but also by their radically different, diametrically opposed features. The road leading to Luvina is uphill, but descends to reach the valley of Comala. Luvina is built upon a rocky, desolate mountain ridge, where the barren soil cannot support its inhabitants and the crop it yields is barely sufficient to keep them alive. The soil of Comala is fertile, but there is no one to till it. Barren nature kills off the inhabitants of Luvina, turns them into living dead; in Comala it is the dissolute human community that lays waste the fertile land. In this respect the two works seem to represent the complementary halves of the same circle, approaching the same problem — existence made impossible — from opposing sides. It is not surprising that Rulfo identifies both villages with hell, or purgatory, the scene par excellence of human suffering in the literal sense of the word.

The nameless narrator says of San Juan de Luvina That name sounded to me like a name in the heavens. But it's purgatory. (13)

And the carter Abundio, before they reach Comala, explains to Juan Preciado

That town's the hottest place in the world. They say that when somebody dies in Comala, after he arrives in Hell he goes back to get his blanket. (14)

20

Though for different reasons, the climate of both villages is equally intolerable: either too cold or too hot. At all events the implication is the same: these are places where life is impossible.

The short story and the novel both lead the reader into a void, surrounding him with an identical sound environment. Here the silence can be heard and all sounds are mute. The sounds are not originated by living beings but by plants, the wind, by disembodied spirits. The plaintive moans do not issue from human throats; the cries of pain that can be heard are the cries of existence bewailing its suffering. This is why there is no escaping the validity of the lament. The effect of the sound environment is further heightened by the sultry, oppressive climate. There is not enough oxygen to breathe in either village.

It was impossible to calculate the depth of the silence that shout [the shout of a village ghost] created. As if the earth had been emptied of air. No sound, not even the sound of my breathing, or my heart beating. (15)

says Pedro Páramo. And to the traveller heading for Luvina the nameless storyteller says

A little before dawn the wind calmed down... But there was a moment during that morning when everything was still, as if the sky had joined the earth, crushing all noise with its weight... (16)

To his wife's question: what is this noise, the man replies

It's the silence. (17)

There is no life without air to breathe, just as there cannot be human existence without words. In these villages the inhabitants are suffocating as though they

were being choked. Death chokes the breath out of Juan
Preciado, though he is young and there is no indication
of his being ill upon arrival in Comala. His death has
no physical cause. The process taking place in his
consciousness manifests itself as inanimate reality:
there is not enough oxygen in the air, too little of
this indispensable substance reaches his lungs. But it
is not primarily the body: more than anything else, it
is the consciousness that suffers. Rulfo presents this
damage of the consciousness not as a psychic phenomenon
but as a material loss caused by the external world. As
we have seen, Rulfo's method is to represent the human
in the sphere of the inanimate, and to endow the inanimate with human characteristics. Juan Preciado dies for
a subconscious cause turned material, exemplifying the
transformation of a mental phenomenon into a material
one: he is killed by the climate of Comala. In other
words Rulfo represents the social environment, which
naturally has a tragic effect on Juan's consciousness,
as sound and atmospheric conditions, thereby objectify-
ing it. He uses a climatic code to formulate social
experience.

The impression of these places being purgatory or
hell is further strengthened by the absence of light.
The narrator of the short story first meets the inhabitants of Luvina at night; and upon his arrival to
Comala Eduviges leads Juan Preciado to her alleged
quarters through a maze of dark rooms. The absence of
light and the effects of sound together evoke the image
of hell and those suffering there

> Well, I went to the plaza and leaned against one of
> the pillars in the arcade. I could see there wasn't
> anybody there, but I still heard the murmur of

voices, as if it were market day. It was just a
meaningless hum, like the sound the wind makes in
the branches of a tree at night, when you can't see
the tree or the branches but you can hear the rustle.
Like that. I didn't go any farther. I began to sense
that muttering coming nearer and circling round me
like a swarm of bees, till I could finally make out
a few words: 'Pray to God for us.' (*18*)

The murmur of voices, sounds that do not issue from
moving lips and chill Juan Preciado's soul (he says to
Dorotea: "You're right, Dorotea. It was the voices [in
Spanish, the murmuring] that killed me." (*19*)) we asso-
ciate in our minds with Dante's Inferno and Ulysses'
trip to the underworld.

The protagonists of both the short story and the
novel consider their experiences to be of universal
validity. As there are young and middle-aged narrators
in both, this generalization relates to the whole of
human existence. We have mentioned that in both works
the goal of the journey is the familiarization with the
way of life in a certain village. In Luvina the narrator
poses the following question to his wife

What country are we in, Agripina? (*20*)
and the significance of the question is signalled by his
posing it again

What country is this, Agripina? (*21*)

As a consequence of the connotative meaning of the
word the journey of discovery is directed at much more
than a single village — it aims to discover, to get to
know the whole of Mexico itself. Juan Preciado is shocked
by Comala, he too is incapable of understanding, of
realizing all that happened to him there, but even Pedro

Páramo is unable to penetrate Susana San Juan's world, forever incomprehensible to him.

The author's concern for the fate of his country resounds in the question: what country is this? He is shocked by the impossibility of creating an existence in this land, which is true of the barren heights of Luvina as it is of the fertile valley of Comala. Luvina is

... a dying place where even the dogs have died off, so there's not a creature to bark at the silence (22)

and Comala is peopled by ghosts.

There is only one possible answer to the narrator's question: This is the country of death.

Juan Preciado's adventure with the woman whose body was made of earth and made as if to dissolve into a puddle of mud points in the same direction

I felt [says Juan Preciado] as if I were drowning in the sweat that streamed from her. I couldn't breathe. (23)

Who is this woman, molded of earth? Her incestuous relationship with her brother is a consequence of that total seclusion that is sometimes an appurtenance of destitution. This episode, which could be taken from real life, surpasses the boundaries not only of Comala, but also of Mexico, for it revives those ancient myths in which woman is the primal matter who creates the world through conceiving by her brother. Through this earthen-bodied, incestuous woman Juan Preciado recognizes the essence of material, perishable, fleeting yet eternal human existence. The recognition of this essence deals him a fatal blow; with the dissolution of the woman's body the world itself dissolves, vanishes and with it all Juan Preciado's hopes. The destruction of his hopes inevitably results in his death, in relation to which we have already received many hints. For example, a deathly tiredness overcomes him when he arrives in Comala; little by little the strength, the will to live leaves him.

The narrator of the short story was able to return from the village of Luvina, but he returned too late, for, as he says, "Luvina gets you down". (24) (In the original, this read: Luvina finishes you off.)

The lives of both protagonists — like the earthen--bodied woman's — disintegrate, become worse than nothing, turn into non-existence, eternal unrest, from which there is no respite even though one of them no longer lives in Luvina and the other (Juan Preciado) is dead. The eternal unrest of non-existence torments the one--time inhabitants of Comala like it does the villagers of Luvina, arousing in them an avid hunger in the literal and in the figurative sense of the word: in both villages the people are starving. In Luvina they are starving because there is not enough food to go round; in Comala because the ghosts cannot liberate themselves of their insatiable hunger for a free and happy life without privation even after death. Their hunger is whetted by their anger over their misspent lives, for not one of them, not even Pedro Páramo, who made a fortune, ever attained that which he most desired. Pedro Páramo is long since dead, yet the author still names him "ever--present hate", vindictive malice. Continuing the drawing of the parallel between the inhabitants of the two villages: in Luvina hunger turns the living into shadows, while in Comala unremitting bitterness does not allow the dead to die. Once more short story and novel represent the two halves of the same circle.

Their diametric opposition is apparent in their geographical location. Neither village is situated at what can be considered the average height above sea-level in Mexico: Luvina is placed much higher, Comala much lower than the average.

> Sometimes the road went up, sometimes it went down: They say a road goes up or down depending on whether you're coming or going. If you're going away its up-hill, but its down-hill if you're coming back. (25)

This exceptional location, differing as it does from the average, provides the traveller setting out to discover himself and the world above all with a new perspective. The confines of everyday life rob man of perspective: the customs of one's environment, the prejudices and conventions of those coming from the same region enslave and blind. By his estrangement from the level natural to him, because of the extreme height or depth at which he finds himself, the vision of the traveller is sharpened, his horizon expands. He perceives the essence of things much more clearly, his judgement is more resolute, more sharp. This double perspective, the gaze directed at the world from the heights of Luvina and the depths of Comala ensures the spatial completeness of the received image, enables one to consider it from all aspects. The alienation from everyday life makes it possible to penetrate the core of Mexican life and society, and to recognize there the misery of man in every sense of the word.

Only bitter fruit grows in the fertile valley of Comala, and it would be a vain effort to look for fruit, or even flowers, in Luvina. Bitterness and barrenness, physical and spiritual hunger distort life into purgatory and hell in these complementary pieces of fiction.

Juan Rulfo's family moved South from a cold, mountainous region. The village where they made their home soon ceased to be the lively commercial centre they found upon arrival; its inhabitants left the neighbourhood and the heat and the drought soon turned the country-side into a wilderness. The story of his family, which he scoured after with the avid hunger born of the sense of being uprooted, and displaced that strikes those orphaned at an early age and brought up at an orphanage repeatedly led him back to these opposed poles of misery. The inhabitants of the mountains, sunk into silence, and the ghost-villages of the low-lying, torrid plains appear time and again in his works. During one period of his life his occupation involved continuous travelling. Like the protagonists of his books, he too was always heading for a place only to depart from it without ever finding a true home.

The height and depth of Luvina and Comala, his wandering heroes and the perspective deriving from the geographical differences of level are therefore all nourished by the author's personal experiences. Rulfo emphasizes that it is reality, Mexican reality that he wishes to portray, to relate. But did the ghosts of Comala truly speak to Juan Preciado?

His compassion, pain, despair and impuissant desire to help transform the world which he perceived from his own creator's perspective with the sensitivity of an artist and the wider knowledge of the intellectual into a tormenting personal vision. He is the traveller who dies in Juan Preciado and he becomes as one with the ghosts of Comala who can find no rest on this earth. This is why the rich Pedro Páramo is no exception – he too becomes one of the many miserable people who have been robbed of everything and can find no meaning, no aim to life.

This exemplarily realistic novel, written in the last century, illustrates the richness of life through its variety of characters. The author's attitude is naturally manifest in this plenitude, but the collectivity of characters does not display it. The author either comments upon his own tale or he entrusts one of his characters with the expression of this attitude, with the enforcement of it. The victory or the defeat of the just can transmit his world image equally.

If we may speak about models in contemporary Latin American fiction, we can do so because the author does not attempt to present a wide scale of human personalities, nor endeavours to outline an extensive social panorama arising from the inequality of their condition, but is content to seek the similar, that which is identical in them all, and which points definitely to his world image, as well as to what can be expected if this world image not only proves to be valid, but also if it proves to be the *only* valid image of the world, and shall remain that. The traveller will either be encaptured, engulfed by the netherworld, or, as it happens in Luvina, shall return without having effected his purpose and live a make-believe life from then on. What a departure from the original topos! The traveller has no trials to undergo, has no need to prove his superiority, and no kingdom awaits him at the end of the journey. The absence of action, the dissolution into nothingness, or the return to the point of departure without being given the possibility of even attempting a trial makes time unreal in these novels.

We have come to a standstill in Mexico (26) says Rulfo. Timelessness is a consequence and a symbol of this deadlock. It is quite obvious that there are forces at work in Mexico also, striving to accelerate social development. But there is no place for them in Rulfo's work, for in the end it is his own vision that he wishes to project before us in a model of the world that is protest itself.

x x x

The world image unfolding from Rulfo's oeuvre, in accordance with his declarations, is determined by a sense of social responsibility. It would be futile to search for philosophical inspiration in his work; every event, every episode attests that the author's attitude is nourished by experience, according to which the overwhelming majority of Mexico's population lives in ignorance, in appallingly backward circumstances, and there is little hope that these circumstances, the economic and intellectual poverty it suffers, may be relieved.

The short story and novel under analysis unfold along the lines of the basic myth-tale-plot (Ulysses, the young man trying his fortune). The dénouement, however, differs from the original formula — contradicts it in fact. In consequence, it is not the eternal human significance of embarking upon a journey that it exemplifies, but the hopelessness of such a venture.

Besides the mythical element that undoubtedly plays a role in the plot, it is the system that sets the narration into motion within the geographical, thermal and sound-climate relations, the paradox of high and low, cold and hot, noise and noisy silence (scratching plants and muttering dead) that strikes one. These alternatives are intended to make perceptible, in an unequivocal way, the totality of experienced reality. Whichever direction the author chooses to make his approach from, the conclusion is always the same. The similarities of the personae are also destined to encourage the drawing of the same conclusion, and are thus more significant, more meaningful than any existent psychological, physical or social difference could be. Thus the collectivity of characters may be grasped as a single, communal character. This fusion of individuals also seems to confirm that the despair is total and does not depend on the individual traits of any given character.

The time of the action is necessarily unreal if the tale is spun from the web of reminiscences told by ghosts. For that matter, Rulfo does not reveal the date of Juan Preciado's arrival to Comala, nor does he specify when the village had become deserted. The rustic environment lends itself particularly well to the perpetuance of the feeling of timelessness, for it changes but little in the course of centuries. We cannot know the age the travellers to Luvina live in, and the fact that it is not the journey of he who is heading for the village, but that of he who is returning from it that is related connects the course of events with the image of a closing circle, and through this ties it to the timelessness of perpetual repetition. The moment initiating the narration merges into the circumvolution; it cannot be connected except to the commencement of another cycle, further enforcing the emphasis laid on the *inescapably always the same*. Both in *Luvina* and in *Pedro Páramo* the moment that *launches* the narration is occasioned by nostalgia, and in the novel, where the young narrator dies and the title hero-narrator who lived to a great age comes forward with his own childhood reminiscences, it is not only impossible, but needless and without interest to determine the exact time of this moment, for it links up naturally with the endless cycle of human life lasting-from-birth-to-death. Compared to the presumable total time of the action, the time of the narration is extremely short in the novel as in the short story. Yet this rate is contradicted by the laborious course of the individual episodes which do not in effect comprise the action proper, relating meditations, interior monologues or dialogues concerning past events instead. Nor is the original action the immediate subject of the short story — its subject is the account of this action, told as a monologue (or a dialogue in which one of the participants is always silent) which necessarily entails a prolonged time of narration, as it is in principle the total reproduction of a delivered speech.

It is obvious from all this that Rulfo was successful in eliminating the enormous differences between the duration of the action and that of the narration, for instead of a brief summary he relates the events in the form of reminiscences or dialogues, submerging the reader into the sluggish, almost still waters of monologues and dialogues. This sluggish quality, which naturally also creates an impression of timelessness, is furnished by a multitude of parts intended to appeal to the senses, by the repeated portrayal of climatic effects in the wider sense of the word. The description of an act of perception accomplished in a split second naturally requires a longer period of time than the act which it relates, just as the accounts of the yearnings and reminiscences of the village ghosts, which are condensed into a single, if recurring moment.

The essential trait apparent in every character — the unsatisfied or thwarted craving for life — assures in itself the high frequency[*] of these works. To this is added the repeated occurrence of certain fragments of speech and statements and, above all, the recurrent description of the climatic effects to be understood in the previously expounded sense of the word.

Leisured narration and high frequency does not for a single moment, release the reader from the grip of a hopelessly, eternally identical world.

---

[*] Frequency (the recurrence of certain elements of the novel) as interpreted by Gérard Genette; for more details cf. *Mario Vargas Llosa.*

Notes

Juan Rulfo

(*1*) Juan RULFO: *The burning plain* (Llano en llamas).
     Transl. G.D. SCHADE. Univ. of Texas Press, 1967. 120.
(*2*) Juan RULFO: *Pedro Páramo*. Transl. Lysander KEMP.
     Grove Press Inc., New York. 1.
(*3*) *The burning plain*. 112.
(*4*) ibid. 112.
(*5*) ibid. 114.
(*6*) ibid. 116.
(*7*) ibid. 113.
(*8*) ibid. 118.
(*9*) ibid. 118.
(*10*) ibid. 119.
(*11*) *Pedro Páramo*. 6.
(*12*) ibid. 9.
(*13*) *The burning plain*. 120.
(*14*) *Pedro Páramo*. 3.
(*15*) ibid. 30.
(*16*) *The burning plain*. 116.
(*17*) ibid. 117.
(*18*) *Pedro Páramo*. 57-58.
(*19*) ibid. 56.
(*20*) *The burning plain*. 115.
(*21*) ibid. 116.
(*22*) ibid. 120.
(*23*) *Pedro Páramo*. 55.
(*24*) *The burning plain*. 120.
(*25*) *Pedro Páramo*. 1-2.
(*26*) "En México estamos estabilizados en un punto muerto."
     Luis HARSS: Juan Rulfo, o la pena sin nombre. In:
     Recopilación de textos sobre Juan Rulfo. In: *Casa
     de las Américas* No. 18. (1969). 1.

II. JUAN CARLOS ONETTI

Kierkegaard and Onetti

The existential character of the Uruguyan Juan Carlos
Onetti's world image is revealed by his first short
novel, entitled *The pit* (El pozo). There is only a few
months' lapse between the publication of this novel and
that of Sartre's *La Nausée*, generally held to be the
first existential novel. The distance between the two
countries and the short time lapse between the two pub-
lications preclude the possibility of the French writer-
philosopher's influencing Onetti. Despite this, literary
theory has made no attempts to discover the origins of
his existentialism. In his study of the French and Latin
American nouveau roman, Leo Pollmann points out that we
cannot identify the Latin American authors' existential
cast of mind and awareness of life with Sartre's existentialism taken in the literal sense of the word.

Nothing can be farther from the Latin American
writers' intentions than to place their works in the
service of that philosophical trend of thought, bearing the imprint of Cartesianism, according to which
existence precedes the essence. They are not in the
slightest degree concerned with a theory which ex-

plains "Everything" and conforms to concrete reality
in accordance with philosophical reasoning. (1)

Pollmann emphasizes the consciousness of rootless-
ness as the essential element of existentialism as is
manifest in Latin American fiction. Discussing *The pit*,
he excludes the possibility of searching for a philosophical model in this work — as we might do in Sartre's
case. The hopelessly isolated protagonist, living symbolically in a pit, does not live segregated from his
fellow men

> ... because existence for Onetti would mean isola-
> tion (which would be existentialism), but because
> his eyes cannot see the beauty of the world, which
> naturally exists. (2)

In Pollmann's opinion, Onetti speaks of a particular,
specific human destiny,

> ... to which corresponds, according to ancient Span-
> ish custom, a certain morality of universal valid-
> ity. (3)

The inconsistency of this statement is obvious. If the
specific case is the medium of a universally valid morality, the accusation that it is incidental and does not
contain a mature authorial conception is unfounded and
false. The consistency of his approach as appears from
his oeuvre is sufficient confutation of Pollmann's
statement in itself.

A more intensive study would not only demonstrate
the existential character of the oeuvre, but would also
question Pollmann's other supposition, according to
which the existentialism of Latin American authors is
instinctive and does not result from philosophical reflection. This surprisingly inaccurate judgement of
Onetti probably derives from the fact that for Pollmann

Sartre's type of existentialism is the standard. The strongly speculative character of this type of existentialism is in effect opposed to the attitude of Latin American authors, acquired through their comprehensive experience of existence. Though Pollmann does mention Kierkegaard in passing in connection with Asturias, he does not notice that the roots of Onetti's *Weltanschauung* originate in and are nourished by the works of the Danish philosopher.

A brief life furnishes sufficient proof of this. Some of the pages of the chapter entitled *Los desesparados* (The despairing) correspond almost word for word with a number of Kirkegaard's arguments in *The Sickness unto Death*. Kierkegaard speaks of the despair of the weak and the despair of manliness, Onetti of the weak and the strong. According to the Danish philosopher, the weak always appears to be more desparate than the strong because the weak is unable to bear the weight of his despair. This weakness drives him to seek help and to expect deliverance from a source or event independent of him.

> In [the despair of manliness] there is now a mounting consciousness of the self and hence a greater unconsciousness of what despair is and of the fact that one's condition is that of despair. Here despair ... does not come from without as a suffering under the pressure of circumstances, it comes directly from the self ... to hope in the possibility of help ... he will not do ... rather than seek help ... he would prefer to be himself. (4)

In *A brief life* one of the characters speaks of the "pure" despairer, whom he has never had the fortune to meet, though he has been waiting for that chance all his life. (In the Bible it is Job who personifies the pure des-

pairer). Apart from this, undiscoverable, pure despairer
there are only impure weak and strong desperate men — he
says

> Because apart from what I will now describe, there
> is nothing more to the weak or strong desperate man:
> one is subordinate to his desperation and the other,
> without knowing it, is above it. It is easy to con-
> fuse them, to mistake them, because the second, the
> impure desperate man, passes through desperation
> but is strong and superior to it; it is he who
> suffers the more of the two. The weak desperate man
> shows his loss of hope with each act, with each
> word. The weak desperate man is, from a certain
> point of view, more lacking in hope than the strong
> one. Hence confusions arise, and it is easy for him
> to be deceived and perturbed. Because the strong
> desperate man, although he suffers infinitely more,
> will not show it. He knows, or is convinced that no
> one can console him. He does not believe in his
> ability to believe, but he has the hope, he, the
> desperate man, that in any unforeseeable moment he
> will be able to confront his desperation, isolate
> it, see its face. And this will happen if it suits
> him: he can be destroyed by this confrontation, he
> can reach grace by it. Not holiness, because such a
> state is reserved for the pure desperate man. The
> impure, the weak desperate man, on the other hand,
> will proclaim his desperation with system and pa-
> tience ... he will always be capable of creating the
> small world he needs so as to curl up and get
> drowsy ... There is no salvation, I would say, for
> the weak desperate man. But the strong one ... can
> walk in the world without involving others in his

desperation, because he knows he must not expect help
from men or from his everyday life. He, ... without
realizing it, he awaits the moment when he will be
able to look it in the eye and kill it or die ...
Unfortunately there are no sores eating away at him
from the soles of his feet to the top of his head;
he is not seated on ashes, nor has he been given the
opportunity to kiss the stone on which he scratches
himself ... He will not reach the touching verbosity
of the pure desperate man in the presence of a predestined Elijah the Tishbite... (5)

The quotation makes it obvious that Onetti is thinking
of Job. It is worthy of note that Kierkegaard bases the
work entitled *Repetition* on the Book of Job. His choice,
like Onetti's, falls upon Job, for it is in Job that
suffering manifests itself most clearly and unequivocally, for the precise reason that he does not deserve such
suffering because of his transgressions. In Kierkegaard's
eyes Job exemplifies man's generic misery because his
fate unsurpassably expresses that the human state of
existence is despair. Onetti's reference to Job reveals
that he shares this point of view and proves that the
protagonist of *El pozo* — like so many other Onetti characters — is not living in the pit of his isolation acci-
dentally, is not a unique case, but is a sharer of the
universal human condition.

We shall presently attempt to disclose the similarities concerning the behaviour of the desperate man, the
causes of his despair and the possible modes of deliverance as they appear in the works of the philosopher and
the writer.

Kierkegaard distinguishes three phases of despair.
In the first the despair of man is caused by circum-

stance, in the second man becomes the source of his own despair and in the third despair arises from man's confrontation with eternity.

> The despairer ... transforms something earthly into
> everything earthly ... Recognizing that he is in
> despair about the eternal, he despairs over himself
> that he could be weak enough to ascribe to the
> earthly such great importance, which now becomes his
> despairing expression for the fact that he has lost
> the eternal and himself ...
> Man, when he is confronted with himself, enters the
> sphere of the eternal, but this eternity is not
> identical with God. Only after having recognized the
> eternal quality of his conflict does he recognize it
> as a conflict between God and himself. (6)

In *A brief life*, the wife of the protagonist Brausen undergoes a mammectomy. As a result of the operation, the man loses all desire for his wife, his love for her dies, their life together is wrecked. This first phase, the primary motive for despair, is rarely described by Onetti. He presumably considers the communication of the event engendering despair an unnecessary anecdote. He generally presents his characters in the second phase, when they have themselves become the source of their despair. Brausen enters the second phase when he acknowledges that the fault lies with him — there is not enough love in him to surmount the difficulties of the present situation; and the image he had of himself collapses. From here he arrives at the third phase as a matter of course, extending the validity of his new awareness of himself onto the whole of the human race. Brausen, like all the other Onetti characters, betrays that he has reached the third phase of his despair by

seeing life — not only his own, but in general — as
meaningless. Though all Onetti characters are convinced
of this, their every thought and deed is performed in the
hope of finding a way out of the trap of meaninglessness
— a hopeless struggle, which they are aware of. Kierkegaard characterizes the man in the throes of despair in
the following way

> His despair is that of weakness, a passive suffering
> of the self ... he makes an effort ... to defend
> himself ... and his despair is ... not willing to be
> himself. On the other hand, the ludicrous notion of
> wanting to be another never occurs to him ... As
> long as the difficulty lasts, he does not dare to be
> himself ... he comes to himself only once in a while,
> as it were on a visit, to see whether the change has
> not occurred... (7)

The change of personality, this recurrent motif of
Onetti's works, is the desperate attempt of the despairer, in conformity with Kierkegaard's analysis, to
liberate himself of his insufficient self and thereby to
perfect, to make whole this imperfect, fragmented self.

Brausen, having proved insufficient, wanting in love,
is unable to continue living his accustomed life and
attempts to recreate himself by assuming new personalities. Under the assumed name of Arce he has an affair
with a prostitute, because he wishes to achieve perfection in depravity, if in nothing else, and creates a
whole fictitious world for himself in which he reaches
the summits of wisdom and resignation in the guise of a
fictitious personality, Díaz Grey. In Kierkegaard's
words, he

> ...loves to think that this change might be accom-
> plished as easily as changing a coat... (8)

At the same time, as Brausen, he returns to his old
life every now and then as if to see whether some sort
of change has occurred that may deliver him from the
trap of despair. The characters of Onetti's other novels
all make attempts to extricate themselves from this trap
— he has a predilection for the word — through a change
of personality. Larsen of *The shipyard* is another who
escapes into a fictitious personality: he plays the role
of managing director in a factory that has long since
ceased functioning. For that matter, almost all the characters of the novel are playing parts: this is the most
effective means of survival. These actors by necessity,
driven to the peripheries of society can expect nothing
from circumstances, from their surroundings; their despair and search for a way out of the trap manifests itself in their refusal to be themselves, however ridiculous they may feel their play-acting to be. The protagonist of the novel entitled *Let us allow the mind to
speak (Dejemos hablar al viento)*, chief of police Medina
also changes his role: he becomes a night nurse, then a
painter, then a chief of police.

In Brausen's, Larsen's and Medina's case alike, the
change of personality takes place in order to assist
them in their discovery or creation of their real and,
at the same time, more complete, more perfect selves.
Kierkegaard sums up this tendency in the following words

>After all this you feel that the most important thing
>is not the refinement of your intellect but the ma-
>turing of your personality. (9)
>All three characters are over forty,
>... at the age when life begins to be a twisted
>smile (*10*)

their despair confirmed and made final, unchangeable by
their experiences, by a long succession of failures.
Their roles make it possible for them to start life anew
and to try out other possible modes of behaviour. But in
actual fact each role is a repetition of the next in
that they all lead to the same conclusion.

This repetition, like the changes of personality, is
a method, a means of extricating oneself from the pit.
Kierkegaard expresses the essence of this attempt thus:
the despairer

> ...discovers that there is something he must perform
> again, something he must evoke again, and for the
> most part this is very difficult ... For here applies
> what the fairy-tale recounts about a certain enchant-
> ment: the piece of music must be played through back-
> wards; otherwise the enchantment is not broken ...
> this is the only way to tear the ingrained defi-
> ciencies out of the individual, and every consequent
> error implies that one must begin the whole process
> anew. (*11*)

The attempts of Onetti's heroes are all aimed at the
elimination of chance, of the false steps that decide
human fates; at the discovery of that point and place in
time when their life or they themselves failed; where
life inevitably and unaccountably took a wrong turn. This
is why they depart and return, expressing by this change
of location that they are searching for a new personality
only to retrace their steps along the old tracks in the
hope of repairing the past.

Brausen entrusts the repairing of the past to his
imaginary persona, Díaz Grey; before his death, Larsen
creates a new future for a young boy, wishing to evade
through him the indignities he had to suffer in his

youth; the unrealised alternatives of Medina's life are
fulfilled by the alter ego of his youthful self — his
son. Their despair, like true despair, is irresolvable,
final. According to Kierkegaard it is

> ... the sickness unto death ... the torment of des-
> pair is precisely this, not to be able to die ...
> not as though there were hope of life; no, the hope-
> lessness of this case is that even the last hope,
> death, is not available ... This [is the] sickness
> in the self, everlastingly to die, to die and yet
> not to die, to die the death. (*12*)

True to the Kierkegaardian concept, despair is the
manifestation of the unfulfilled death-wish, the un-
realized suicide for Onetti as well. Nevertheless, the
despairer dies the death every day; his life is an endless, everlasting process of dying.

Brausen, Larsen and Medina are incapable of committing suicide, though they have lost all sense of value
and in consequence all hope. Others commit suicide in
their stead: Elena Salas, a figment of Brausen's imagination; Gálvez, Larsen's accomplice in the play-acting,
and Medina's alleged son. As the extract from *A brief
life* proves, the meeting with the pure desperate man becomes a desired but never realised miracle. The despair
directed at the self originates in the impurity of the
self, and despair is a universal human condition because
no one is pure.

Both Onetti and Kierkegaard consider purity the utmost redeeming value, though Onetti's conception of purity does not coincide exactly with Kierkegaard's, who
saw chastity as the embodiment of purity according to
the ideals of the nineteenth century. But Onetti, too,
finds this value in a young girl, though it is not her

body, but her mind that is untouched by the squalor and filth of the age: by self-interest and moneygrubbing. This idealized young girl — as Onetti is well aware — is an ephemeral miracle, but still she is the symbol of a demand asserted *ad absurdum,* a demand that is therefore of a philosophical nature. It is characteristic of the philosopher and the writer alike that they both project this demand upon the individual, expecting the resolution of the problem of existence to be signalled by the destruction or the redemption of the individual.

Man doomed to despair by his mode of existence is unable to redeem himself either by a change of personality or by repetition. To escape the confines of the trap, Kierkegaard turns to divine grace, but Onetti expects man to solve his own conflicts. Instead of throwing oneself on the mercy of God he proposes that one should trust in existence. Brausen reconstructs a night of his youth in his mind

> I would have declared positively, alone or before
> the deaf, that the period of perfect life ... the
> days made to the measure of our essential being —
> that this period of perfect life is attainable ...
> if we know how to abandon ourselves, to interpret
> and obey signs of destiny; if we know how to despise
> what has to be obtained with effort, what does not
> fall into our hands through a miracle. All the knowl-
> edge of life ... is in the simple delicacy of ac-
> comodating ourselves to the gaps in events that we
> haven't provoked with our will, in not forcing any-
> thing, in simply existing each minute... (*13*)

Neither Kierkegaard nor Onetti gives an intellectual answer to the question as to whether there exists a possible way out of despair, which they both consider the universal condition of the human race. According to both, the solution would be the living, the experiencing of something, of divine grace or of existence accomodating itself to existence, but determination or resolution does not assist the individual in either attempt. The self should attempt everything in order to find the key to itself but should finally surrender itself: this is the advice of both Kierkegaard and Onetti. The philosopher found a solution, if only for himself, in the form of divine grace, but Onetti is fully aware of the impracticability of his solution: life cannot be rectified in the way that he proposes.

Character drawing

The significance of character-drawing in the narrative literature of the last century and the beginning of this one is remarkable, regardless of whether it is romantic, realistic or psychological novels that are in question. Though to somewhat varying extents, every character is the product of his inclinations and/or the influences social circumstances exert upon him. The author is fully aware of the likely actions and reactions of his characters, of every tremor of their heart. The enlightenment bequeathed a deep respect for rational thinking and science to the nineteenth century, and this respect was further deepened by positivism. In his famous *La Comédie Humaine* (The Comedy of Man) Balzac's professed intention was the scientifically thorough revelation of human nature, while Zola in his cycle of the *Rougon-Macquarts* carries out what might almost be called laboratory experiments in order to prove the accuracy of the laws of contemporary genetics.

Philosophy, sociological theories and the development of technology and science all left their mark on the narrative literature of the last century. The authors believed in the unlimited possibilities that science offered and, stepping into the shoes of the scientist capable of solving any problem — existing, let us add, only in their most cherished dreams —, created a world whose every rule they knew by heart. It is thus that they became the omniscient creators of narratives based on the principle of causality.

When the great era of the novel ended, the narrators lost their sense of security, found it more difficult to orient themselves in their fictitious world than their predecessors had done; logics failed not only in face of the actions of the characters, but also in face of the circumstances themselves. It has long become a truism to say that the bourgeois social system became unstable, insecure; in this general atmosphere of insecurity and instability the sciences dealing with man adopted a rather cautious attitude. A new trend appeared in psychology: that of behaviourism. The sciences that influenced the narrative literature of the last century underwent a change, but their new aspects are still determinative in relation to the literature of today. Besides social circumstances, which unquestionably play a primordial role, we must also take into account that men of letters have always reacted sensitively to philosophical, psychological, sociological and other scientific theories, which naturally also reflect the given social conditions. These theories are expressed not only in the image that authors form of the world but also in the forms that their works assume. Without behaviourism we would be hard put to explain Juan Carlos Onetti's method of character-drawing, though it is obvious that it is mainly the method (description confined to the registration of the perceptible) and not the *why and wherefore* of the characters that may be attributed to the influence of behaviourism.

According to E.M. Forster (see the series of lectures published in 1927 under the title *Aspects of the Novel*), the protagonists of any novel are either flat or round, depending on whether they can be summed up in a word or sentence or not, or depending on whether they are capable of actions or reactions not easily integrated with the image one has formed of them, and thus capable of causing surprise to the reader.

Though Forster's criterion in all probability cannot be related to Onetti's personalities, I shall nevertheless attempt to apply it in the hope that it will reveal something of them and of their role in the modern novel.

Once again it is *The Shipyard* that I take as subject for analysis. The gestures and words of the protagonist Larsen are, as we have seen, calculated, theatrical, striving for effect. How can we judge him, how can we love or hate him? For, according to Robbe-Grillet, this is precisely how a character should affect us; furthermore

... he should have a name; two, if possible: a family and a Christian name [Larsen has only one]. He should have parents from whom to inherit certain traits [We know nothing about Larsen's parents]. Should he have some possessions, so much the better. [Larsen has nothing.] He must have a personality, a face that reflects it, a past that formed and moulded him in some way or another. [Our information concerning Larsen's past is minimal.] His character should determine his actions and reactions to any given event. [Even if it is obvious from certain indications that he must be a mean and worthless kind of person, this has no bearing upon his actions.] (14)

As we have seen, Larsen — like all the other characters — imitates standard modes of behaviour. Our next task is to ascertain his motives for choosing the forms that we have traced. He dissimulates, acts a part, but not in the hope of gaining any kind of tangible profit by it: he does not wish to fool even himself. He is not an opportunist, though this would be the rational explanation of his lies and conduct.

The narrator, when he is not one of the already mentioned characters, is for the most part a collective personality, an unnamed "we" or someone who identifies himself with this "we". To this faceless public plays Larsen, Petrus, Gálvez and Kunz. According to Larsen, Petrus

> ...was born to this game, has been playing it since I was born ... I am his brother, tho son and I salute him with respect. (15)

Of Gálvez and Kunz he says

> And they're just as hypocritical as I am. They make fun of the old man, of me, of the thirty millions; they don't even believe that this is or ever was a shipyard ... But every day they climb the iron staircase and make themselves believe that the game is more real than the spiders, the leaks... (16)

Díaz Grey, who occasionally personates the nameless public, ranks himself among the clowns, and considers that this definition of himself holds good of everyone else.

> All of us know that our way of living is a farce, we
> are even capable of admitting it, but cannot change
> it, for each must safeguard his own personal farce
> besides... (*17*)

The definition relating to the individual is made
universal by extending it over every man.

Larsen, aware of his clown's status, knows that his
performance needs a stage

> He thought that the shack formed part of the game;
> that they had built it and were living in it with
> the sole purpose of enacting those scenes which could
> not be performed in the shipyard... (*18*)

The theatre, the enactment of a life never lived but
avidly desired first appears in a short story of Onetti's
entitled *A dream fulfilled* (Un sueño realizado). In the
novel entitled *A brief life* Brausen, who is commissioned
to write a screenplay, invents the little town of Santa
María and the personage of Díaz Grey because it is
through and by this fictitious world that he hopes to
recapture his past and lost happiness. The characters
of *The Shipyard* also endeavour to recreate, to perfect
their lives through the aid of their imaginary world.
However hard we try to identify ourselves with our
imagined personality, it is obvious that it shall remain a simple role for us unless a pathological psychic
change should occur and total identification with the
new personality should engulf the real self.

The greater the differences between the characters,
the more valuable the character-study of the traditional
novel appears. In *The Shipyard* however, as we have seen,
the author does not emphasize the differences between
the characters, nor even their personalities and natural
endowments; on the contrary, he seeks what is similar or

even identical in them. Every male personage can be characterized by the same word, every one of them can be placed in the same category. The clown-comedian (*farsante*) is at the same time an accomplice from the point of view of his relation to other people. While the comedy is being enacted, each pretends to take the other's performance seriously and this tacit complicity assures the continuity of the play. Josefina, Angélica Inés' servant-girl, for whom Larsen feels a brotherly affection, is such an accomplice.

It is characteristic of all the men and women, of every personage in the play that they are marginal beings confined to the peripheries of life. Angélica Inés' mental deficiency necessarily excludes her from society; Gálvez's wife, besides sharing her husband's fate, is cut off from life by her total indifference to everything that is an accomplishment or common ideal of the welfare society: in her shabby man's coat, cumbersome man's shoes she is slatternly, unkempt, her home is more like a kennel than a house.

But neither Angélica Inés nor Gálvez's wife plays a part. Their every word and deed is instinctive, unaffected, natural. They are pure in the sense Onetti attributes to the word, that is, their actions and emotions are not determined by interest. Angélica Inés would be incapable of any such consideration, and Gálvez's wife understands that revenge is more important for her husband than she herself — she makes no objection against his leaving her and taking with him even the money they put by for her confinement. The most fundamental trait of her personality is the simple, spontaneous and natural acceptance of the world and herself. This is what her declaration

I was born and here I am (*19*)
signifies. *Mutatis mutandis* the same holds true of Angélica Inés as well. Opposed to the *masqueradors* who do
not reveal their true selves, Angélica Inés and Gálvez's
wife are authentic.

In *The Shipyard*, in which the individual reacts to
environmental stimuli — or, to use Toynbee's expression,
to the challenge of society — there is no representation of social conditions; the author makes no mention
of the unevadable course or laws of history and society.
The challenge of society is hidden, mute; one can only
guess at its character from the behaviour of the personages. That in relation to which the personages are either
authentic or comedians is a *terra incognita*, a vacuum,
but an extremely powerful vacuum, as the reaction to the
challenge, the behaviour of the characters attests — the
characters who are outcasts, peripheral beings, but who,
turning towards its centre, at the same time form two
complementary halves of a circle, the half-circles of
comedians and authentic beings.

The concealed but present society is as powerful as
a fast current. The characters strive to escape its pull;
their clowning is a refuge from its annihilating force.
Their desperate attempts to continue the game at all
costs is a measure of the destructive power of society.
In consequence the shipyard, the scene *par excellence* of
the play, becomes in a paradox manner the scene of truth.
Those who live here have seen the true face of society
no longer disguised by the comforts and pleasures it more
or less guarantees to those who keep to its rules.

In opposition to this undisguised society, Larsen,
Petrus, Gálvez and Kunz choose the fictitious world of
the theatre; the air of exile which is

...an air difficult to tolerate at first, almost impossible to do without later. (*20*)

It is their play-acting that binds them together. As
we have seen, it is from the charade that they hope to
win fortification. They are all aware that the other's
play-acting is also performed in the hope of fortification. The double aspect of the shipyard is that it is
simultaneously the scene of play-acting and of truth,
and explains why it is the "home" of comedians and authentic personages alike. It is an empty stage which may
be filled with illusions by the actors — or an existence
divested of all delusive ornamentation, where genuine,
authentic behaviour — the disinterested love of Gálvez's
wife — may be born.

It is common knowledge that the nature-image appearing in the first line of Hungarian folk-songs, though
apparently unrelated to the rest of the text, bears symbolic content. Onetti uses a similar resource before revealing to us that Gálvez has left his wife. Larsen's
glance falls upon the wall calendar

That is how he came to know that ... he, and all the
others were living the day of the Immaculate Heart
of Mary. (*21*)

This seemingly insignificant statement foreshadows
and intimates the disinterested goodness of heart and
the love of Gálvez's wife, which is further enhanced by
the next sentence

Everything changed, perhaps because of the name of
Mary ... which he had only just then understood...
(*22*)

and the description of the woman's hair

...the dusty, serrated crown of stiff hair. (*23*)

52

— an obvious allusion to the crown of thorns, symbol of suffering endured out of love.

The other authentic character, Angélica Inés, cannot adjust to the world and to its questionable value judgements because of her mental deficiency. She and Gálvez's wife embody the extreme poles of unselfish, disinterested behaviour. Both are capable of disregarding their own interests — Angélica Inés through her total lack of comprehension, Gálvez's wife through her total comprehension.

Opposing them, in the other half-circle are the men representing various stages in role-playing behaviour. Petrus, the most genuine actor of them all, never accepts that the game is over, so his fate seems to extend into the far reaches of eternity. From one of Kunz's accounts, rendered by the communal "we", it is obvious that he too will continue to live on, but for radically different reasons. He resigns himself to the ending of the play as readily as he consented to take part in it. Between these extremes continues Larsen and Gálvez's deadly struggle for existence in the tension caused by the confrontation of the real and the imaginary world, the society that cast them out and the shipyard: the promised land that provides a refuge; and their struggle is deadly in the figurative as in the literal sense of the word.

Their prehistory is not identical. Larsen arrives to the shipyard when he has traversed all the paths of life, when he knows there are no more paths open to him. His decision to remain is the consequence of his awareness of his situation. Gálvez on the contrary feels that he is the victim of Petrus. He does not understand that it was not Petrus but society that laid the trap for him. It is only after he has denounced Petrus and revenged

himself that he realizes that it was the trap of the
shipyard which enabled him to escape the final trap of
society, the unevadable trap of human fate. He who in
his thirst for revenge was so eager and youthful turns
to his past, a past, a youth lived in society to find a
way out of the trap. He realizes his mistake but it is
too late to turn back and he commits suicide. Larsen
does not attempt to return to his old life, and when all
hope for the continuance of the play dies, he sets out
towards old age: towards death — forwards, in a sense.

It is not their characteristic traits that distin-
guish these four personages from each other, but the
nuances of difference in their reactions to the challenge
of society. They are all actors: each can be summed up
by this one word. Their individuality derives from their
particular manner of continuing the selfsame game. Aside
from these nuances of difference, with these similar
types of character Onetti turns the attention of his
readers to the society hidden and unexpressed which
forces each of them to react to its challenge in a more
or less identical way.

Obviously, Forster's evaluation relating to shallow
characters cannot be applied to *The Shipyard*, where the
characters are created with the precise intention of
endowing them with an essence that may be condensed into
a single word.

The personages of Onetti's novels are not true characters in the ethical sense of the word. Their being
noble or base is unimportant. What captivates the reader
in them is the face beneath the mask, which sometimes
allows us a glimpse of its true physical or psychical
aspect, but which always remains fragmentary and mysterious. In their desire to participate in the formation

of their fate (a desire which remains unfulfilled), if only through play-acting, they are very individual indeed; and very universal, for it is their desire to fight that counts, not their individual traits.

Onetti's characters are memorable because they are mysterious, because behind their visible and minutely described masks their real faces appear for moments only, and mostly because we feel that we are somehow contained within their existence, and thus unperceivably become as one with them.

As we have seen, the characters form a circle around a black patch: society, which remains undescribed; and in relation to this society, they are either actors or authentic beings. This black patch, this vacuum spins them around like a whirpool, and it is in seeking to escape it that they situate themselves on its outer edge. The whirlpool sucks Gálvez down into its depths — upon his return to society, he commits suicide — and casts Larsen far out into non-existence, upon finding that the play is over, he sets out towards nothingness, towards death. The inverse currents of the whirlpool keep Petrus forever spinning on its outer edge, and he thus escapes the danger he never acknowledges: the discontinuance of the game. Thanks to his resignation, Kunz sinks slowly and without suffering shock towards the vacuum at the centre of the vortex, in other words, returns to society gradually, step by step. The women too get caught up in one of the concentric circles, doomed to remain peripheral beings due to their lack of comprehension or too profound insight, which allows neither to become a part of the given society.

The condensing of the characters into a single word thus leads us to the structure of *The Shipyard*. Any transverse section of this structure reminds us of an amphitheatre. This is well suited for play-acting; especially the stage, which on the surface of the story is the shipyard, but on a deeper level of the structure is society itself. What we must realize is that the relationship of the characters and the audience is inverted and society is not only a stage but a leading character in this novel, despite the fact that it remains concealed and unexpressed throughout, gaining shape only in the reactions given to its challenge.

Every section is by necessity static, yet the structure of the whole, despite the slow progression of events, is based on the functional principles of the vortex, and this dizzying spinning does not end even with the last words of the novel because of the differences in degree within the same reaction.

(The character study of a single novel naturally cannot be conclusive. But it may assist in the more precise drafting of certain questions.)

A fundamental difference between the traditional and the modern novel is that the first attempts a direct portrayal of reality while the second undertakes to create a possible model based on the author's experience of reality. (To be sure, this does not apply to all of the above-mentioned novels, only to a certain, presumably the greater, part of them.) Fundamentally, the subject of the modern novel is not social experience, but the attitude or point of view abstracted from it.

This difference must naturally find expression in character-drawing. Direct experience entails the description of the interior and the exterior, the physical and the mental characteristics of the personages. In the case of narratives based on such a type of portrayal,

the more versatile the personages, the better the novel,
by necessity.

When an attitude or point of view becomes the subject of the novel, the characters are not portrayed
directly, but, similarly to the practice of the traditional novel, must harmonize with the subject, that is,
must be in concordance with the point of view it expresses. This concordance demands that the essential
traits of the characters must crystallize in the retorts
of the abstraction, and must be as model-like as the
entire world of the work of art is model-like.

It would therefore be a mistake to expect round
characters, but it would also be a mistake to underrate
their significance, for they are — as far as can be inferred from the example of *The Shipyard* — important, and
often decisive factors of the system activating the narrative.

In medieval abstractional literature, the figures
embodied abstract ideas. In the long run, actor and
authentic being or, in other words, the false and the
real may also be qualified as abstract concepts. Yet it
seems that while the medieval figure embodying a concept
had only a conceptual and not a live relationship with
the other characters, and was a conceptual creation, as
was the work of art itself, the figures of the modern
novel are born of the abstraction of relations. Their
negative or positive relationship to each other, deriving from the nature of the society they are depicted
against bears evidence of the author's image of the
world, as their conceptuality condenses the essence of
this relationship.

In a traditional sense these characters have no personality, and social conditions do not appear in the

novel either. Characters and surroundings blend into an apparently inseparable and indistinguishable mass.

Behaviourism was originally created out of the social necessity of increasing the efficiency of human labour in the knowledge of the likely modes of behaviour subject to the given environmental stimuli. And yet Onetti, who confines himself mostly, though not exclusively, to the depiction of the visible and the tangible in his character-drawing, sets before us individuals who are incapable of adapting to society. Understandably, he does not attach too much hope to the development which should have elevated Uruguay to the ranks of the welfare states. Though he gives no voice to his opinions or judgements in relation to this, through his personages, portrayed according to the unevadable rules of behaviourism and reversing this trend to oppose his own original aims, he reveals to us the darkest side of society.

x x x

The characters do not only give us the key to the system activating the narration, but also reveal that Onetti's image of the world, based primarily upon existential philosophy, comprises an unexpressed, not easily discernible, but all the more significant social experience, and a judgement formed on the basis of it.

In consequence, the method discloses certain traits of this world image that cannot be found either in the statements of the author, nor in the plot, nor even in the opinions and commentaries of the characters.

Like in Rulfo's works, there are many mythical elements in *The Shipyard* that may be applied in the deciphering of the message. Jaime Concha's reference to the connection between Petrus's house as a temple and the glorieta's candles, to the liturgic quality of the novel is accurate. (24) In my study entitled *Razones y características en la obra de Faulkner, Rulfo, García Márquez y Onetti* (25) I too have mentioned that Petrus' house fulfils the role of the Saint of Saints; it is the gateway to Paradise. This interpretation allows us to draw a parallel between Rulfo and Onetti. If Rulfo implied through atmosphere that the earth is hell or purgatory because we cannot realize our dreams or desires on it, then Onetti, by not allowing Larsen to enter Petrus' house — he can never get further than Josefina's quarters, can never get up to the first floor where Angélica Inés and Petrus live — is also formulating the impossibility of fulfilling human desires. This interpretation, however relevant, does not reveal the entire spectrum of Onetti's image of the world.

Onetti's characters, as we have seen, can be reduced to a common denominator, resorting as they do to identical patterns of behaviour; the differences are only in their past and in their future, forecast by the dénouement. Like Rulfo, he too seeks the identical in his characters, who may therefore even be considered a collective or communal character.

Onetti's specifications of time, "five years later", "at five o'clock" etc. are all aimed at making the action verisimilar. At the same time, however, this action cannot be dated, for it can be co-ordinated to any fifty years of our century. The characters feel that they are participants in an always identical scene. The course of the action is not progression: it simply goes round and round. Larsen, before his death, experiences the same sensation in Josefina's arms that he recalls from his

youth: the cheap taste of life. This conclusion gives
the impression of a circle closing in upon itself. The
author blurs the differences between past, present and
future and strives to condense all three into a single
moment in time. Paradoxically, besides and despite the
specifications of hour-time and periods of time implying
genuine passage of time, he makes the action float in an
unreal time, in which he is assisted by the make-believe
quality of that action. The game that replaces life
naturally takes place out of time, in a vacuum where
there is no time, and the action is as unreal as time
itself.

As unreal as is the scene, the factory which is no
longer in use, where the workers have no longer anything
to work on. Placed into parentheses, detached from real
life, the action has no content in itself; we can only
speak of a few months of occurences if we step out from
between the parentheses, return to Santa María or leave
the shipyard for ever.

Though we know very well that Santa María is also
the product of the imagination of a character in a previous novel, this fictitious world nevertheless seems
sufficiently real for us to compare it with and in comparison judge unreal the action taking place in the en-
chanted atmosphere of the shipyard.

The moment initiating the narration cannot be placed
in any sort of calendar chronology. As in the case of
Rulfo, here too this moment can be attached to a journey,
or rather, to a specific situation. Someone arrives to a
certain place because he wishes to get to know something,
to face something. In *The Shipyard*, the event initiating
the narration is death; this is what Larsen must face,
this is what lies in wait for him and catches up with

him upon his final departure from the shipyard. Between his arrival to Santa María and his death succeeding his departure from the shipyard there is nothing but the game of make-believe, placed in parentheses. The removal of the parentheses — to continue this mathematical metaphor — does not change either the situation preceeding or following them, depending on the mathematical symbol or sign of operation we add to it, for the game, the play-acting, must always equal zero in the real world of the action. The calculable difference of speed between the duration of the action and that of the narration is great for reasons similar to those relating to *Pedro Páramo*. Every section repeats monologues, not events. In principle, these monologues are equal in duration to those originally uttered, while the summaries naturally demand more time than the original glance, perception or process of thought, the duration of which is extremely short, and hardly, if at all, calculable. In *The Shipyard* as in *Pedro Páramo*, a high frequency is coupled with leisured narration, for in the behaviour of the characters, as in the situations they find themselves in, parallels and repetition are the rule.

The negligible action, like the monologues is used primarily to conceal an inevitable process: the approaching of death, and Larsen's patient and attentive waiting directed towards it.

Apart from a tell-tale sentence dropped every now and then, the point in question is always beside the question. Our study has demonstrated this in relation to society, but starting from the point initiating the narration the same may be said of that aspect of the novel relating to individual problems of existence. The authenticity but undatableness of the moment initiating the narration signals the genuine and at the same time universal validity of this problem of existence.

Notes

Kierkegaard and Onetti

(1) Leo POLLMANN: *La "Nueva Novela" en Francia y en Iberoamérica*. Gredos, Madrid, 1971. 65.
(2) ibid. 88.
(3) ibid. 88.
(4) Søren KIERKEGAARD: *Fear and Trembling* and *The Sickness unto Death*. Princeton University Press, Princeton, New Jersey. 201.
(5) Juan Carlos ONETTI: *A brief life* (La vide breve). Transl. hortense Carpentier. Viking Press, New York, 1976. 194–195.
(6) S. KIERKEGAARD: *The Sickness unto Death*. 195.
(7) ibid. 188–189.
(8) ibid. 187.
(9) S. KIERKEGAARD: *Either/or*. 101.
(10) J.C. ONETTI: *A brief life*. 45.
(11) S. KIERKEGAARD: *Either/or*. 103.
(12) S. KIERKEGAARD: *The Sickness unto Death*. 150–151.
(13) J.C. ONETTI: *A brief life*. 227.

Character drawing

(14) Alain ROBBE-GRILLET: *Pour un nouveau roman*.
(15) Juan Carlos ONETTI: *The Shipyard* (El astillero). Transl. Rachel CAFFYN. Charles Scribner's Sons, New York, 1968. 97.
(16) ibid. 52.
(17) ibid. 90.
(18) ibid. 75.
(19) ibid. 134.
(20) ibid. 165.
(21) ibid. 165.
(22) ibid. 144.
(23) ibid. 144.
(24) Jaime CONCHA: El astillero. Una historia invernal. In: *Cuadernos hispanoamericanos* Nos. 292–294. (1974). 554, 562.
(25) Katalin KULIN. Recursos de la creation mítica, Faulkner, Onetti, Rulfo, García Márquez. In: *Annales, Sectio Philologica Moderna*, Budapest, tomus 6. (1975).

GABRIEL GARCIA MARQUEZ

Mythical motives

Many episodes based on events familiar from history
can be found in *One Hundred Years of Solitude* by the
Columbian Gabriel García Márquez: the thousand days' war
between the conservative and liberal parties, represented
in the novel by Colonel Aureliano's thirty-two unsuccessful campaigns, the influx of capital from the United
States — the banana company that radically transforms
Macondo's way of life, bringing with it a significant,
though temporary, prosperity; the massacre succeeding
the labour strike of 1928, evoked in the novel by the
dark line of wagons transporting the dead bodies of the
strikers, gunned down in the square in front of the sta-
tion. The way in which Macondo's inhabitants live in itself characterizes Columbian reality.

Despite this, the historicity of *One Hundred Years
of Solitude* does not derive from the detailed description of Columbian political and social events, but from
the perspective "transcription" of the country's specific and peculiar conditions, which makes it possible for
other peoples to recognize in them their own situation
and conditions.

Columbia — as the whole of Latin America — did not develop autonomously, for the Spanish conquest destroyed the modes of production till then in use, leaving only a few scattered Indian agricultural communities, and in their stead originated peculiar relations of production, the likes of which Europe had never known. The colonies geared themselves to production for export, and though there was no home market characteristic of feudal modes of production, the relationship between producers and purchasers was essentially feudal in character. The Spaniards paired mercantile economic principles with feudal — or even ancient if we think of slavery — relations of subservience.

These complex forms of production determine Latin American development even today. This is the reason why the question as to whether there is feudalism or capitalism or a medley of both in Latin America today still gives rise to much controversy.

The gaining of independence was immediately succeeded — in some places, even preceded — by the influx of foreign capital, which in the last century entailed a chiefly economic dependence, and which in our age, due to the absolute economic influence of the United States, has come to mean political dependence as well.

The black-garbed lawyers of *One Hundred Years of Solitude*, who in the time of Colonel Aureliano sold their liberal allegiance in exchange for parliamentary positions and the monies that go with these are the legal advisers of Mr Brown, the director of the banana company who will stick at nothing, and the representatives of state officials, Latin American intellectuals bribed by the United States. The American influx of capital and export of profits, the organized charities and the agreements concerning these, which transform subsidies and grants into sources of profit for the capitalists of the United States — all these led, in an increasingly obvious manner, beginning after World War II, but especially after the revolution in Cuba, to a political and military dependence.

The anachronisms of the novel — though they may seem the consequence of the arbitrariness of the author to those accustomed to European historical categories of development — are in fact nourished by non-autonomous Latin American development. Economic, political and military dependence — in other words, neo-colonialism — puts fetters on Latin America, makes healthy development impossible. This abnormal development, the *subdesarrollo,* constitutes the grounds of García Márquez's conviction, voiced to a reporter of the *Prensa Latina* in 1971

> I believe that our history is a *circulus vitiosus,* within which even the names never change; our structures are gone to ruin, for they have spun round so many times that their reparation is no longer possible; in time they will go from bad to worse and the only solution that remains is the wind of destruction that will tear everything out by the roots so we may start from scratch once more.

This statement, incidentally reinforced by many other successive interviews, casts light upon the social-ideological attitude that fundamentally determines García Márquez's image of the world. In 1969, also to a reporter of the *Prensa Latina*, he says

> I consider myself sufficiently developed ideologically and perceive the world accordingly.

An analysis of *One Hundred Years of Solitude* will presumably confirm that his method corresponds to his

image of the world. In this novel we found that the
system activating the narrative is the system of myths,
which we have attempted to disclose on the basis of the
following definition

> A myth is a sequence of fragmentary events, the sys-
> tem and meaning of which is determined by the recol-
> lection of a given historical period of the beginning
> and the end.

For want of space we do not undertake to elaborate upon
this definition, but refer to the chapter entitled *What
is Myth?* of the article published in 1972. (*1*)

The beginning and the end — the concept determining
the fragmentary events — is the foundation, then the
destruction of the "city", the socially organized human
community. The fragmentary events that may be considered
the fundamental units of *One Hundred Years of Solitude*
must therefore be interpreted in their relation to the
"city" as a historical process. Their significance is
determined — distorted — by the foundation and destruction of the city — that is, the "city" must be considered the key to the novel, it is to be thought of as
a message in code. In our definition we have pointed out
that it is a given historical period that recalls the
beginning and the end. Though we omitted to enlarge upon
the present, as a historical period, we do affirm that
in *One Hundred Years of Solitude* García Márquez creates
a myth that is characteristically Latin American and
which portrays a generally twentieth-century manner of
posing questions.

In the ascending section of the novel there are many
who assist the author's protagonists in their ventures.
José Arcadio Buendía does not set out to seek a "new
home" alone; he is accompanied by young people with whom

he founds Macondo and who subsequently accompany him on his expeditions. Colonel Aureliano, who joins the army of the liberals, goes to war alongside his friends, and José Arcadio Segundo is assisted by hosts of organized labourers. The ventures of all three are doomed to fail only when their companions fall behind and they are left alone.

It is at this point that the message of the novel, applying to Columbia and Latin America, gains universal validity. Márquez portrays the abnormal condition common to Columbia and Latin America, but he penetrates the core of the disease and by doing so touches upon a problem that is characteristic of the twentieth century.

We refer to the fact that the historicity of a myth derives from the experience of "something is wrong", an experience that is inseparable from a concrete, given age. If this assertion is correct, then we must know Columbia, Latin America and the twentieth century to a certain extent in order to understand the experience of "wrong" that inspired the Marquezian myth.

Seeking the fragmentary events and the units into which they are grouped, we must begin with those that are mythical in character. In this we are justified by the method of the author, who, simply by making use of mythical elements, qualifies the customary devices of narration as insufficient and inadequate. This is presumably due to the recognition that the generally known signification of mythical fragmentary events compels the reader to attempt to interpret them without any particular directions to this effect, while the distortion of meaning caused by the concept of the foundation and destruction of the "city" simultaneously forces him to modify his evaluations.

The mythical event-units therefore necessarily have a double meaning, or even several meanings (the given mythical element undergoes a change of meaning in the various myths — that is, it imparts a content inexpressible by simple, logical communication and in consequence its use is at the same time proof of its indispensability). It is self-evident that the elements indispensable to the communication of the subject must be placed at the focal point of the literary examination.

The two decisive "prehistorical" events preceding the foundation of Macondo — the "city" — and determining the new period are the marriage of Ursula Iguarán and José Arcadio Buendía, her cousin, and the killing of Prudencio Aguilar.

Translated into the language of myths, an incest and a murder.

Both elements can be found in various kinds of myths from all over the world, and as such they are "invariable", that is, particularly well-suited for the imparting of a message that may be received anywhere.

Incest is taboo and considered a mortal sin by all societies alike; the only difference of opinion concerns the degree of propinquity at which it is permissible or strictly to be forbidden. Though inter-tribal marriage is compulsory in endogamic societies, sexual relations between the son or daughter and the recognized ascendant is forbidden even in these communities.

We do not know the exact degree of propinquity between the first couple of *One Hundred Years of Solitude*, but we do know that the two families have been intermarrying for hundreds of years. The congenital defect of Ursula's uncle is a consequence of endogamy. The parties concerned are aware of this: the practice of endogamy must be stopped; it jeopardizes their chances of healthy offspring, threatens their hopes for a healthy future. The marriage of the Buendía couple is incestuous according to the developing new principles rather than the practice of the society to which they belong.

The other "invariable" element is murder. Jose Arcadio Buendía kills Prudencio Aguilar. The evaluation of this mythical element is by no means as unequivocal as that of the previous one. For one, it is the source of the greatest evil, chaos, violence that brings death; for the other, it is the source of cosmic order, the creation and preservation of human life.

In Assyrian and Babylonian myths, for example, the young god must vanquish all the gods representing chaos — without distinction of good and evil — in order that cosmos, an ordered universe, may be born out of chaos; in Hindu and Greek orphic myths the god kills the titan or titans to create man from the remains — from the ashes of their cremated bodies; in South American Indian myths it is from the buried parts of the goddess's body, sacrificed by humans, that the crop springs up and grows.

The relation between the above-mentioned fragments of action is that of cause and effect. To avoid committing incest, Ursula and José Arcadio Buendía do not "consummate" their marriage. This leads to the murder of Prudencio Aguilar, his killing being a murder of retaliation for his derisive taunts. To escape committing another murder, the couple commit incest.

Of the two "prehistorical" mythical elements — the original murder (2) and incest — García Márquez utilizes only one, that of incest, for the end, the recollection of the destruction of the "city".

This is a natural consequence of the unambiguity of this element and of the ambivalence of the original murder. The fall of the "city" — of society — cannot be connected to an event which — like the original murder — contains the germs of a certain creative process despite its negative quality.

If we consider the identical motifs of the designators of the beginning and the end — those that pointed from the beginning to the end, towards destruction, it is incest and within the notion of murder, it is the killing, the simple fact of destroying another human being, that we must think of.

Both incest and murder calls for a primarily ethical type of evaluation.

We have, however, seen that in ancient myths murder does not appear on an ethical level — even if we relegate the evil it implies to that level, an act that is in itself questionable — but is a communal, social, historical act.

We have emphasized that a myth is the recollection of a given historical period of the beginning and the end, and as such it is not exact truth, but a valid truth.

Considering incest and murder as harbingers of destruction and dissolution from the vantage of the twentieth century, it is obvious that it is the factors determining the historical process which must be sought within them. This is why their ethical or psychological aspects are not pertinent: they denote only in so far as they are valid from the vantage-point of twentieth century historical experience.

This historical experience — as we have already affirmed — can be summed up by the term of "something is wrong". If we then examine incest as the denoter of this "wrong" that shapes the concept of the beginning and the end, it becomes obvious that it should not be considered from the angle of sexual depravity or inversion, an angle that the author himself ignored. Ursula never thinks of her marriage as immoral or perverse, and the same may be said of Amaranta Ursula and Aureliano's love.

In both cases the only reason for concern is the possible birth of an abnormal child, a freak — essentially, it is the future, continuance: what next and how? that is endangered. We may therefore establish that this mythical element signals the immanent danger of human existence made impossible.

Its purpose as such is evident in Amaranta's case as well — she also rejects her cousin's proposal of marriage for fear of the child that may be born. The virgin Amaranta's sexual flirtations with Aureliano José and José Arcadio assure that this mythical element, connected with the beginning and the end, is kept permanently on the agenda as it were, so that the "spectre" of incest forever haunts the Buendías.

Incest is a constant denoter of the process that takes place between the beginning and the end — that is, the process is itself human existence made impossible, though this becomes manifest only at the end of the novel, embodied by the freak that is finally born.

Amaranta's much too timid and gentle heart is unconquerable. Isn't it strange that neither Pietro Crespi, nor Colonel Gerineldo Márquez — by whom she is deeply attracted — can touch her innocence, but she engages in dubious adventures with her cousins, for whom she feels no affection? Assuredly it is not strange —

moreover, it explains what was that one attribute of incest that made it García Márquez's most suitable choice for the conveyance of his message.

Members of a family are all familiar to each other, never different enough to seem strangers; being a member of a family always means some kind of identification, an alikeness that is expressed by the identical names. A Buendía in the arms of another Buendía is not the coupling of two independent beings, the victorious disruption of the boundaries of personality, the assurance of the possibility of human co-existence — it is the self protected by itself, the individual ensconced in the safe haven of its own boundaries, a never endangered solitude.

It is possible — or so it appears from the relationship of Aureliano and Amaranta — that incestuous love is the absolute realization of the ancient desire of "becoming as one", but this total merging is not a true victory because it derives from identity, from sameness, and does not involve the necessary dynamics of the striving for an almost unattainable goal — is not an example of human co-existence radiating hope.

If we were right in our evaluation of the role of the denoters of incest, if the destruction of the "city" distorts this mythical motif by making it represent solitude out of all the possible interpretations, then the negative aspect of the original murder may be decoded in a similar manner: If I kill the other person I shall be alone.

But the usage of both elements at the same time betokens a certain dissimilarity, else one of them would be superfluous. Incest remains within the sphere of individual life, while murder affects the whole community:

to continue the thought *ad absurdum*, murder will result in solitude, for there will be no one to live with if we exterminate our possible partners.

Solitude is not necessarily negative, or, more exactly, its evaluation varies according to the given age.

The hermits seeking seclusion in the desert strove to achieve meditation of the highest order in solitude; a number of the romantic poets sought escape from the society that depraves and destroys natural life in solitude, which for them signified a purer, more sublime way of life.

Consequently, the contextual value of the mythical elements relating to solitude depends on the historicity of the concept, that is, on the experience of "wrongness" of the given historical period. It is obvious that the twentieth century experience of "wrongness" — which identifies the historical process lasting from the beginning to the end with the process of human existence becoming impossible, and which chooses as denoters of the process only such mythical motifs as can be interpreted as the mythical transcription of solitude in consequence of the distortion of the concept — can only be alienation. Alienation in the widest sense of the word, that is, a process which corrupts individuals in their relation to themselves and others, a process which impedes direct and indirect social development.

To come to the hitherto undiscussed positive aspect of the original murder: in *One Hundred Years of Solitude*, the killing of Prudencio Aguilar is the direct cause of the foundation of the city.

In the lives of the Buendías and the Iguaráns, which has been following the same pattern for centuries, remorse over the murder — which the author, by embodying it as it were in the ghost that comes back to haunt them, divests of its psychological aspect, strange as this may seem — remorse, then, is the beginning of the process of their awakening, of their awakening awareness of themselves, the beginning of human culture.

The origin of the feeling of "something is wrong" is at the same time the origin of the struggle for something "right" or good. The Marquezian myth would be meagre indeed — or perhaps would not even be a myth at all — if it portrayed alienation simply as the disease of our age without showing its positive historical significance. Especially if it declared man to be a failure, unfit to do battle.

The process that starts at the beginnings of time, though it is the process of human existence becoming impossible, at the same time comprises the struggle against this process — that is, comprises the struggle for the perfection of life as well. This much is evident from the knowledge of the end.

The most significant, most ancient and at the same time most modern feature of the Marquezian myth is that the source of "good" and "evil", of life and death, is the same — the original murder — for mankind takes time to rationalize its basic experience and to confer these to two different gods, or to God and man; and it may be considered most modern because it makes man and only man the source of good and evil, that is, vests him with the dignity of total responsibility.

For simplicity's sake, we have used the terms "good" and "evil", though — as we have already pointed out in relation to incest — the Marquezian attitude is not ethical. It is not good and evil that does battle for the domination over the Buendías; their actions are not evaluated from an ethical point of view by the author: the sole criterion of any act is whether it forwards or hinders the development of the "city".

This does not mean that the individual is important only in relation to the community. Incest, as we have seen, is destined to denote the solitude of the individual. The original murder would have sufficed, had García Márquez been interested solely in the social aspects of life.

Action as a criterion may be applied in the case of the individual as well. Desolating solitude is as tragic for the individual as it is for the community. The relation between the two is obvious. Our attempts to differentiate between individual and communal life was made in order to point out how equal they are in value in the novel.

If we attempted to make an ethical evaluation of the characters, we would find that there are some who are "better" and some who are "bad" but this would run counter to the author's intentions. García Márquez shapes his characters with equal affection and sympathy, and even the most selfish of them cannot arouse the aversion of the reader. We instinctively sense that their fate is to share in the self-same tragedy: they cannot find a way to each other.

Alienation is a standard subject in contemporary literature. But we must recognize that it depends on the concept of the work in question whether it offers no more than the mere symptomatology of alienation in conformity with the author's total social adjustment (as in the nouveau roman), or whether it contains elements that point beyond the limits of the alienated society.

The psychological — or rather, psychopathological — portrayal of alienated man, the realistic description of the symptoms of alienated society, executed with the minuteness of a documentary, is no concern of García Márquez's authorial attitude. Despite his impersonality as a narrator, García Márquez does not perform anatomical examinations on a corpse, does not dissect his characters, but traces man's path towards alienation in the living course of history, within the action itself.

In the knowledge of the denouement of the novel: the destruction of the family, the city, the human community, one may well ask why this method is better than others if it does not only disclose the disease but also reveals the death that it causes, thereby extinguishing the last spark of hope.

It is indispensible to mention here the inexplicable but indisputable opinion of readers in general, their relating of their reading experience of *One Hundred Years of Solitude*. According to them the novel does not arouse feelings of depression or despair — what is more, it radiates, in a most mysterious manner, strength and reassurance.

It is this "mysterious manner" that the last, so far undiscussed factor of our definition: recollection — shall cast light upon.

We have said that the designator or denoter and the designated find shape in recollection, which, as the recollection of a given period, determines the system and meaning of the myth. The meaning of the myth derives not from any type of recollection, but from the recollection of a given period relating to certain events or actions, given that the meaning is always a result of interpretation, and interpretation being the activity of a par-

ticular consciousness — in this case, the consciousness
of a specific period — and contingent upon factors mould-
ing that consciousness.

The system itself, however, is not connected to any
specific consciousness, either because it exists outside
the consciousness, or because the consciousness of man
as a species is suitable for the creation of systems.

The capacity for systematization, therefore, does
not depend on the given historical period (though naturally the degree of perfection that may be attained
changes in the course of history).

The system is the totality of the processes, in co-
operation with each other. Therefore, it is recollection
— in which the process evolving between the beginning
and the end, the fragmentary events, and the process of
recollection itself constitute a close unity due to their
modificatory influence upon each other — that creates
the system of myths.

The functional invariants of the system are therefore identical with the aforementioned characteristics
of the stream of consciousness of recollection: unres-
trained action, revival and enforcement of past processes, unity and totality.

At the end of the novel, the Buendía family dies out
and the whirlwind wipes out Macondo. The effect of this
on the reader — which is contradictory in this instance
— is the result of the recollection that constitutes
the system of the novel.

The author — and with him the reader — never identifies himself totally with the Buendías, who fail in
their undertakings, who are doomed to fail because of
their solitude — for the writer and the reader the "I
can do it" assured by recollection is as real an experi-

ence; the power that allows us to retrace the fate of
mankind — a possible, but not inevitable fate, an assurance that is enforced by the fact that fate is represented by only one family in the novel — that power is
the guarantee of our domination over death, over fate,
over time.

We may turn time back as we like, we may expand the
limits of our lives from the beginning to the end with
the total appropriation of human history, with the
actualization of every moment of that history, with the
realization of completed, perfected future in the concept of the beginning and the end that we may almost
claim to have accomplished ourselves.

The complex interplay of the processes in recollection does not "mirror" life horizontally, but appears to
reproduce it comprehensively, in space, as it were. And
we are ourselves participants of this life, while in
the recollection our independence and, in final analysis,
a possibility for another sort of fate, is given to us.

The recollection being intentional, its consequences
are: he who recollects identifies himself with and at
the same time alienates himself from this life; he recognizes his fate and desires to choose another.

This intentional character of recollection makes the
meaning itself ambiguous: alienation comprises the cat-
egoric imperative of the contention against alienation.

In *One Hundred Years of Solitude* the inhabitants of
Macondo suffer two blows of fate: they are stricken by
the disease of sleeplessness and scourged by the rain
that lasts five years.

The disease of sleeplessness — apart from the fact
that as a blow of fate it can be connected with the ele-
mental calamities and plagues appearing in myths and

symbolizing the wrath of the gods — apparently has no
mythical precedents.

But the disease leads to forgetfulness and forgetfulness has been interpreted in mythical thought. According to Mircea Eliade

The true sacrilege is the forgetting of the act of
God. The fault, the sin, the sacrilege is not to re-
member, for the present, valid form of human existence is the result of an act of God. (3)
— given that the recollection of the original act, the
actualization of it, is the guarantee of the renewal of
existence.

The inhabitants of Macondo, afflicted with the disease of sleeplessness, forget the names and the meaning
of things, are unable to recognize people, and little by
little lose all consciousness of their own selves.

Their forgetfulness makes them incapable of planning,
of building a future, of maintaining any sort of contact.
There is no possibility of communication between those
who have fallen into mental torpitude. The disease of
sleeplessness therefore results in total solitude.

As with every mythical motif used by García Márquez,
this affliction also bears a meaning that differs from
the original. In every myth a sinful act precedes the
calamity that befalls the committer of the sin, the
calamity being a reprisal of the Gods for the sin committed. Essentially this means that wrongful behaviour
is punishment itself, for the omission of duty is ir-
reperable.

Projecting these mythical motifs of calamity upon
the "city", the crime and the punishment for the crime
is the failure to establish a community. This mythical
motif therefore stands exclusively for solitude in the

novel, and would bring to an end the story, life itself, if Melquíades's magic potion did not save Macondo in time.

The origin of the cure is significant and must not be left out of consideration. From the beginning, the function of Melquíades is the establishing of relations, the creation of contact: it is he who brings news of the world and who arouses the desire to relieve the isolation of Macondo in José Arcadio Buendía. It is he who must cure those suffering from the disease of sleeplessness, for what they need above all is a community, contact with others.

In the second calamity that befalls them — the model of which is the deluge, the mythical scourge *par excellence* — it is as impossible to separate crime and punishment as it was with the disease of sleeplessness.

In this case, however, there is a doler-out of punishment: Mr Brown enacts the role of the mythical, revengeful deity — but the act for which he doles out punishment, the strike, is not a crime. Irony and bitterness commingle in the fact that Mr Brown is the only god of García Márquez's world, the absurdity being that anyone may form a right to place himself above a fellow human being, and the bitter reality being that this absurdity can so often and so easily be met with in human relationships.

The strike for which Mr Brown lets loose a deluge upon the inhabitants of Macondo is not a crime. The only possible crime is that of forgetting about the strike. José Arcadio Segundo, returning from the train transporting three thousand dead, finds that no one credits his experiences. The woman whose house he enters looks upon him commiseratively

'There haven't been any dead here', she said. 'Since the time of your uncle, the colonel, nothing has happened in Macondo.' In three kitchens where José Arcadio Segundo stopped before reaching home they all told him the same thing: 'There weren't any dead'. (4)

Forgetfulness and the deluge strike Macondo simultaneously. There is no way of establishing precedence between the two. Here, too, crime and punishment coincide. Forgetfulness — an unpardonable sin according to the myths — descends upon Macondo and overpowers it for the second time.

Thus the responsibility for everything that happens does not fall solely upon the economical and political influence of the United States, but falls also upon Macondo, whose inhabitants escape into facile and easeful oblivion from the troubles befalling them, and do not prepare to put up a fight for their future. In the end they accept their fate, are in fact happy to return to their original state of a hundred years hence thanks to the rain. Mr Brown's deluge would not have sufficed to destroy Macondo in itself; for this, Macondo's acquiescence, its submission was necessary.

Under the influence of the concept the original meaning of the mythical motif changes once again. The rain symbolizes the isolation, the seclusion of Macondo from the outside world. This is why the rain does not trouble Fernanda, who has brought with her the science of living life as if one were already buried from her parental home, and who thinks that

... after all, her whole life had been spent as if it had been raining. (5)

Thus it is once more solitude that is manifest in the motif of the deluge, the impossibility of making contact, of establishing relationships.

This deluge — contrary to the deluge of the Bible — strikes deservedly nevertheless for having forgotten the strike; all Macondo survives the deluge, but none of the survivors deserve to survive. This rain that lasts almost five years is a reversed flood: its function is not to wipe out a corrupt and depraved world, and instead of leading to revival it leads to ruin.

Thus the concept of the city modifies the denoters (incest, murder, disease of sleeplessness and deluge) in such a way that they all come to stand for solitude. The true subject of the novel is not the story of a family, but the problem of solitude.

If we wish to decipher the message of the novel, we must effect an abstraction on another level in which solitude, that is, the subject, assumes the role of the concept. The intentional character of the subject as concept is aimed at the frustration-realization of man's desire for companionship. It is not connected to a given period of the past or the present, but concerns the prevalent present, and thus its historicity — as a message — is valid.

In consequence of the incest and the original murder, José Arcadio Buendía and his wife leave their birthplace. In this episode the elements of two biblical myths are combined, the expulsion from Paradise and the flight of the Jewish people from Egypt.

In the original myths God is an active participant in these events, it is he who drives out Adam and Eve and it is he who delivers the Jewish people from the land of Egypt, whereas in *One Hundred Years of Solitude*

82

man's fate is in his own hands. It is José Arcadio
Buendía who decides to leave his homeland. His departure
may be conceived as an expulsion from Paradise because
he committed a crime: he killed his friend, Prudencio
Aguilar, in retaliation for an insult. But his departure
may at the same time be considered an escape, a libera-
tion, for it is through it that he escapes the ghost of
Prudencio Aguilar.

This last interpretation becomes particularly sound
when the abandoning of their homes becomes final. For
José Arcadio Buendía and his wife do not set out on their
journey alone. They are accompanied by several young
couples from the village. During their protracted wandering they suffer many trials and tribulations — like the
Jewish people while they wandered through the desert. It
is true that their Moses leads them towards the "non-
-promised land", but Macondo is not the land of promise
only in so far as no one promised it to its founders,
and doubtlessly promises no less plenty and affluence
than the land of milk and honey.

But the fact that Macondo was not promised to those
heading towards it by the powers that be does have a
certain significance. It attests that García Márquez
remains completely within human dimensions. The basic
conflict of existence does not take place between gods
— as in certain myths — nor between God and man — as
in the Bible for example; it is man who must create order
out of chaos.

From the vantage-point of the twentieth century, the
exodus is an entirely human enterprise, set in train by
human actions and directed towards exclusively human
aims: towards the creation of a finer, better life.

In its commencement solitude is a significant factor — the expulsion from Paradise signifies among other things that Adam and Eve are left alone, left to themselves, are deprived of their communion with God; in *One Hundred Years of Solitude* the travellers must leave the established human community, but their goal is the victory over solitude, for the foundation of the city, the creation of a better life is a pursuit that takes place on a social level, and the establishment of a community can only be the result of such a pursuit and on such a level.

We are aware, however, that when this goal is placed in position in the sequence of events of the novel, it is fractionally and impermanently realized. Fractionally, for those partaking in the exodus wander lost and lonely in the jungle, far removed from other people, and impermanently, because even after the foundation of Macondo they are still unable to adapt, to become integrated with the great human community, the society of the world.

At all events, by making the abandoned and the sought after "Paradise" a human community, García Márquez makes man responsible for his own fate, and endows him with the dignity of unshared responsibility.

In his dream, José Arcadio Buendía sees a city, and when he asks its name, he hears a word that he has never heard before, a word that has no meaning

...but that had a supernatural echo in his dream: Macondo. (6)

We do not know who replies to his question, and it is obvious that no one is interested in establishing their identity. Even the word "supernatural" does not relate to them, but to Macondo.

The designation of living quarters or the church in a dream is a well-known motif of myths. These places become sacred through the revelatory presence of God or an angel (as the location of the burning bush in Moses's case, or the place where Jacob fought with the angel).

In *One Hundred Years of Solitude*, however, the author adopts only the mark of sanctity, and by making the revelator impersonal, in fact ignores him.

In this manner — and by qualifying Macondo as supernatural — he places the sphere of sanctity within the human world: it is the dwelling of man that is sacred, not because of the deity who appears there, but because of the man living in it.

Nowadays the word "sacred" or "saintly" characterizes one who turns his back on the world and deprives himself of the joys of life; one who in his self-denial and renunciation complies with certain moral requirements.

As we have previously stated, the myth is not primarily a vehicle of morality. "Sacred" or "saintly" in the myths signifies strength and invulnerability, in other words, a power that is capable of anything — of healing or killing — and which, contrary to human laws, is inviolable, for he who commits sacrilege never escapes punishment.

"Sanctity" in the myth is a cosmic law, eternal, unalterable. In the human world of García Márquez sanctity is also a law that supersedes all other laws; stronger than morality, it is an indissoluble bond, an absolute value. In final analysis, it stands for all that is valid.

In the twentieth century, when relativity called in question values that had up till then never been questioned, when social changes proved so many truths till

then believed eternal restricted to a given epoch, when
so many obsolete or unforced laws robbed the people of
their faith in the validity and effectiveness of law and
order, when so many fundamental questions concerning
morality arose and demanded re-evaluation, García Márquez,
by applying the category of sanctity to the existence of
man, to man himself, proclaims that man's acceptance of
his actions, is an absolute value in itself. According
to the message of *One Hundred Years of Solitude*, the
struggle against solitude and for the community is valuable in itself — as is human life, which is ever and
always sacred.

In myths there is a close connection between the
place where a man lives and the way in which his fate
turns out. This is why it is a custom among primitive
peoples for the magician or witch-doctor to designate
the location of each house to be built.

There is a similar connection between the state of
Macondo and the condition of the Buendía house and the
fate of the inhabitants of the village and that of the
family. Inside the house Melquíades' room does not only
mirror the Buendías' fate but is also a mysterious focal
point radiating strength. It is in its dusty and timeless atmosphere that the male members of the Buendía
family prepare themselves for life, and it is here that
they return to renew their strength to be able to continue the struggle.

Melquíades' room stands for many things. It is true
that it is always in seclusion that the men prepare themselves for the world or seek shelter from the world between its walls, like José Arcadio Segundo, but it is
also unquestionable that it is here that the children

and the young are girded for life, for the building of
the city, for the sharing of tasks in the community.

It is ambiguous also in the sense that here time
stands still

It was always March there and always Monday, and
then they understood that José Arcadio Buendía
not as crazy as the family said, but that he was
only one who had enough lucidity to sense the truth
of the fact that time also stumbled and had accidents
and could therefore splinter and leave an eternal
fragment in a room... (7)

and still this is the place where time can be reversed,
it is here that the long-dead Melquíades makes his ap-
perance, it is here that he stays alive, and it is here
that the family's long-forgotten history can be recalled.
Because of this, Melquíades' room stands for recollection in the novel and as such is the scene of the eternal
"can do", in other words, the scene *par excellence* of
the myth. (8)

The exceptional function and category of the room is
a consequence of its being the embodiment of the dialec-
tic unity, the harmony built up of contradictions upon
which García Márquez's view of reality is founded.

What Melquíades' room represents in itself is more
faultlessly, more incontestably, more obviously valid
than the other, necessarily fragmentary sections of the
novel which suggest contradictory existence only in their
totality.

Recollection of Melquíades is the key to the building of the city, the establishing of the community.

Melquíades' unconquerable spirit, the profound experience acquired in the life-time that lasted centuries
and his incredible store of knowledge all serve to con-

nect him with those mythical ancestors whose actions are recalled in the rites of ancient religions in which the constant repetition of their names, the evocation of their deeds is the sole assurance for the successful continuation of life.

The room and Melquíades are parts of the mythical course of events of *One Hundred Years of Solitude*: they are not simply forces tending towards the city, but also manifestations of the frustration of these tendencies. Being the denoters of the city as a concept, they bear the double meaning of community-solitude.

Melquíades is the scholar and the teacher, he who seeks seclusion and he who creates contact between people; a buffoon and a creative genius, a man harassed by the everyday worries of life but possessing super-natural powers, immortal (he has lived several hundreds of years) and mortal like the rest.

Essentially, therefore, Melquíades in turn falls short of our expectations, in turn points far beyond them: deserving of irony and esteem alike.

On the level of the message, the room must be inter-preted as the mythical motif of the "saint of saints", or "most sacred". Its meaning is modified by the theme of solitude as a concept in so far as the dwelling of a deity — and as such the source of divine powers mould-ing human fate — becomes the dwelling of mortal men (Melquíades and the Buendías) and the centre of human forces shaping human destinies.

In relation to the message, Melquíades is the deity and at the same time the high priest of the "saint of saints". He symbolizes the dualism according to which man is simultaneously the goal and the vehicle of the struggle of the community against solitude. The subject

modifies the mythical motif of the "most sacred" and
that of the deity-high priest in such a way that the
"sanctity" they "contain" becomes the denoter of human
life convulsed in the conflict of solitude-community.

Several mythical heroes are fused in the figure of
José Arcadio Buendía, a fusion made possible by the fact
that his long life constitutes a significant part of the
sequence of events of the novel. In relation to the
mythical motif of the expulsion from Paradise we saw him
as a transfiguration of Adam; the exodus portrayed him
as Moses and if we think of the original murder it is
Cain that he calls — if faintly — to mind.

But the image that engraves itself most lastingly
in the memory of the reader is the way in which he is
presented during the last years of his life — bound to
the enormous chestnut-tree in the yard of his house. His
powerful stature, extraordinary physical strength, the
daring ventures attempting the impossible in themselves
create a titanesque image. A comparison with Prometheus
is inescapable if we think of the final, piteous chapter
of his life.

The fate of the titan who, though of divine origins,
is subject to the will of deities greater than himself,
is inevitably rebellion, a rebellion that is nonetheless
doomed to fail from the outset due to his inferior rank
in the Olympic hierarchy. This is why the titan is a
tragic figure, and this is why he may be considered the
prefiguration of man exposed to and at the mercy of
powers greater than he.

José Arcadio Buendía achieves titanesque dimensions
because of the ventures doomed to fail in consequence of
the geographical, cultural and political potentialities
of the Latin American continent — in other words, his

titanesque stature is determined not by the order of
magnitude of his ventures, but by the dimensions of the
difficulties to be surmounted, arising from circumstances.

He is not tragic because he is in a subordinate position to the celestial powers: he does not defy these
and so his punishment does not emanate from them either.

According to the original myth, Prometheus committed
a sin by stealing fire and giving to man that which
belonged only to the gods.

García Márquez, however, adopts none of the criminal
aspects of the motif. José Arcadio Buendía is not straying on to forbidden ground when he tries to expand his
field of knowledge in the interest of Macondo, and his
"discoveries" all lead to facts long since well-known in
science. His crime, therefore — if any —, is by no
means identical with Prometheus'. The only "crime" he
can be accused of in relation to his scientific experiments or his expeditions is that while he is obsessedly
striving to catch up with the present and endeavouring
to connect Macondo with the contemporary world, he is
gradually isolating himself until all contact between
himself and the outside world is irreparably severed.

His life — which augured well at the time of the
foundation of Macondo, when he still enjoyed the full
support of its inhabitants, when all his actions were
performed with them and for them — ends in failure, in
the solitude of madness.

The concept of the city, therefore, distorted the
Promethean myth, retaining of it in essence only the act
performed in the interests of the scientific and cultural
progress of Man. It is not the act that incurs punishment, but the too-powerful, devastating desire to realize

one's aims — a desire powerful enough to destroy human contacts.

Essentially, therefore, as a result of the concept of the city, Prometheus–José Arcadio Buendía exemplifies man creating and destroying community and thus — to a slightly more unpropitious degree than Melquíades — he, too, is a manifestation of the community-solitude motif.

On the level of the message, the concept of solitude distorts the myth of the Titan in such a way that his divine origins — in other words his sanctity — are thrown into relief. The saint who sacrifices his life for the life of man sanctifies human life.

The extension of the concept of sanctity to José Arcadio Buendía also finds expression in the fact that he lives the final part of his life insane. It is common knowledge that many peoples revere the insane as they do the saints, for the labile psyche often finds expression through prophecies and revelations proclaimed in a trance, which are then attributed to divine sources. It was believed that the insane maintained a direct contact with divinity and were thus in possession of secret knowledge. And being in direct contact with divinity, they were perforce believed to be sacred themselves.

García Márquez makes use of this ancient belief to emphasize to the greatest possible degree the significance and value of the figure of José Arcadio Buendía through the application of the mythical category of sanctity in the aforementioned manner.

José Arcadio Buendía's death affords Márquez another opportunity to strengthen the impression of sanctity, already implied by his madness. After several years of absence, the Indian Cataure returns for, as he says

I have come for the exequies of the king. (9)

From time immemorial, myths have supposed a close connection between divinity and the king. Either the king is himself divine, or his power was bestowed by God. In consequence, his person is sacrosanct, inviolable. Cataure's words endow José Arcadio Buendía with these fundamental qualities of the original mythical image of the king. Inviolability is naturally a direct consequence of sacrosanctity.

Inviolability is not solely proper to José Arcadio Buendía — it characterizes his descendants as well. No one dares to put Colonel Aureliano Buendía to death, for everyone knows that not a single member of the firing squad would be allowed to survive the execution. Captain Roque Carnicero willingly submits himself to the gun José Arcadio points at him and much prefers to join the liberals than to effect the execution. He is fimly convinced that by carrying out his orders he would be signing his own death-warrant.

When Captain Aquiles Ricardo charges his soldiers to shoot at the escaping José Aureliano, they refuse obeyance and utter the following words

He's a Buendía... (*10*)

Every member of the family is a "prince", like the men of the chosen people, according to the Jewish religion. The ineffaceable cross of ashes upon the forehead of Colonel Aureliano's son also signals his belonging to the chosen people.

The visible sign as a means of designating the chosen is another recurrent mythical motif. In the *Revelations* the just also wear a mark upon their foreheads. This distinctive mark is in essence the seal of the pact made with God according to which man, in return for divine assistance and protection, binds himself to the fulfilment of certain tasks. (As in the pact "sealed" or expressed by circumcision in the case of the Jewish people.) The mission or tasks that must be fulfilled are in the case of the Jewish people unquestionably historical. By implying that the Buendías are a chosen people, García Márquez emphasizes that their mission is to be accomplished on a historical level and at the same time he qualifies the mission as sacred -- transcribed into contemporary terms, as belonging to a higher order of values.

For the destruction of Macondo, García Márquez uses a motif that has certainly been implied if not expressed in the novel. Though there is seemingly no relation between the assumption of the beautiful Remedios and the annihilation of Macondo, the two events are nevertheless connected by their common active component: the wind.

In myths the wind fulfils an always changing role. The hurricane may be a divine manifestation, but the spirit of retribution may also appear in the guise of a whirlwind to smite down upon those who have sinned. Whatever the effect of the hurricane may be, it is always the manifestation of unknown, irresistible forces.

How can the assumption of the beautiful Remedios be reconciled with the world of García Márquez, which is always of human dimensions?

The effect of the wind, similar in both cases, may prove of some assistance in the solution of this question. The beautiful Remedios, Aureliano and his countrymen have all come to the end of their lives. This strange manner of their passing cannot be accidental.

We know that in the biblical myth the prophet Elijah is also transported up into the heavens by the wind. According to the interpretation of the myth, God performed this miracle as an exceptional favour to deliver Elijah from the agony of death.

García Márquez grasps the same opportunity when he puts an end to the lives of his protagonists with a hurricane. Several signs indicate that the author prefers to avoid "killing" his characters.

The author himself uses the epithet holy only with reference to Merciful Saint Sophia, and though the name is rather ridiculous, this woman is in truth a supremely unselfish, self-sacrificing person. Her disappearance spares us the experience of her death.

In the humane world of García Márquez death is unacceptable and irrational, for it violates the sanctity of life. The mythical motif of the hurricane — like the inexplicable disappearances — affords the possibility of eliminating the factuality of death, of expressing the alienness, the strangeness of it through the agent of meaning effective within it, its active component: the unknown.

x x x

The climate plays an important role in *One Hundred Years of Solitude* — think of the long draught and the rain —, and though its characters are individualized, the names and patterns of behaviour recurring from generation to generation all indicate that they are as easily superimposed upon one another as the characters of *The Shipyard*. In their mythical inviolability they are all princes, the sons of the chosen people, and as such can be conceived of as collective heroes. The novel has no nameable, identifiable, ever-present narrator. The narrative is launched by Colonel Aureliano's nostalgic recollection. The nostalgia that awakens in the lonely

colonel is for the past that cannot be recaptured, for
the rare miracle of a life lived intensively. This avid,
unsatisfiable yearning for life resembles the "hunger"
of Rulfo's personages, though arising under different
circumstances. In *Pedro Páramo* also it is nostalgia that
makes Juan Preciado set out on his journey and it is
nostalgia that launches *the narrative*. The road travelled
by the Buendías proves to be as unsuccessful and ends
with death or destruction like it did in the case of
Rulfo's heroes. The hope that nevertheless awakens in
the reader may be attributed to the reviving, strengthen-
ing power of the myth.

The action spans over a hundred years in time, and
the summary of these hundred years, broken from time to
time by short dialogues, is effected at an exceptionally
rapid pace. There is a question that must nevertheless
be answered: Does the nostalgic beginning and the moral
expressed at the end (a family unable to transcend the
boundaries of its solitude for a hundred years deserves
no second chance) not make the narration itself (referring back and finally merging with the documents of
Melquíades, presaging the action) the subject of the
book? If the subject of the novel is the story recorded
in Melquíades' papers and not the sequence of events of
the hundred years, then the time of the narration obviously slackens, for the novel relates in detail
Melquíades' concise summary, which is short enough for
the last Aureliano to read through from the time the
hurricane strikes Macondo until just before it lays it
level with the ground. We cannot definitely say that the
duration of the narration is slow — we have no reason
or right to say it. But we cannot leave out of consideration that the story of these hundred years doubles back

with the strike against the banana company and retraces its tracks to reach the beginning: the non-existent Macondo. Time devours itself and loses its reality. The sequence of events taking place in irreal time is not easily measured with the exact duration of the narration, expressable in the number of pages.

The exceptionally high frequency of the novel is due to the constant repetition of names, situations, personalities, motifs and fragments of conversation. These repetitions direct the course of the narration to spin round and round. The high frequency is in essence a feed-back and as such encourages a slow narration.

With the summaries comprising many events, García Márquez demonstrates the passage of time, while his high--frequency narration confirms that the passage of time brings no changes. Essentially, this contradiction denies the existence of time, for it is only change that assures us of the reality of time.

The method used in *One Hundred Years of Solitude* therefore complies with the image of the world relative to the Columbian/Latin American society that developed in García Márquez thanks to his ideological training: in it, actual time offering the possibility of progress loses its function, for the various societies remain within the same infernal circle, the regimes that re-place each other bring no real changes.

Paradoxically, the rapid narration reminds one of the fact that despite the accumulation of events, no-thing happens. The system built up of mythical elements activating the narration of the novel is able to convey historicity stalled in unhistoricalness.

Gabriel García Márquez

(*1*) Creación mítica en „Cien años de soledad". *Annales Sectio Philologica Moderna* (Budapest), tomus III (1972).

(*2*) Cf. Mircea ELIADE: *Aspects du mythe.* Gallimard, Paris, 1963. 125.

(*3*) Cf. ELIADE, op. cit. 133.

(*4*) Gabriel GARCIA MARQUEZ: *Száz év magány.* Magvető, Budapest, 1971. 321.

(*5*) ibid. 331.

(*6*) ibid. 391.

(*7*) ibid. 360-361.

(*8*) Cf. ELIADE, op. cit. 301.

(*9*) GARCIA MARQUEZ, op. cit. 156.

(*10*) ibid. 170.

IV. MARIO VARGAS LLOSA

Discourse (1)

With its virtually or totally non-existent plot and characterization, the modern novel has taught the modern literary historian to look at once for the Ariadne's thread that allows him to follow the writer's progress and to understand his allusions and intents and his system of recondite correspondences, all this in the hope of discovering a second reading. Symbols and motifs, strange or hardly intelligible digressions, the specifics of word choice and repetitions — all these are signs and aids for him to achieve his aim.

Paradoxically, *Conversation in the Cathedral (2)* faces the literary analyst with a difficult task because its realistic plot and colourful characters convince him that the first reading is the only possible one; that he is moving in a totally transparent world, the only mystery being a thriller-like one, with that, too, eventually elucidated by the writer.

Any investigation of the immediately understandable appears unjustified. If, however, some cause for anxiety remains, calling for further research, it is not due to the writer's misty vision or our inadequate understanding of his message, but to the extraordinary experience

of such a broad social panorama so long after the era of
realism in the novel, at a time when novels can hardly be
called novels at all, concealed as they are behind soph-
isticated codes of world vision and life perception.

Vargas Llosa presents Peru and the life of the Peruvian in the hierarchy of a class society. Although,
socially, his outlook clearly springs from Marxism, he
is no Marxist himself. Nor is his art marked by any
other philosophical trend. He seems to have been fasci-
nated only by those systems of thought which deal with
creative writing.

Accordingly, the secret of his mordernity is to be
sought for not on the levels of plot, character drawing, recondite symbols or atmosphere, but in the discourse of the novel. Our analysis shall largely follow
Gérard Genette's method (3), which we shall simplify or
expand by further viewpoints as and when required by
the specifics of the novel.

1) Who is the narrator?

The first task facing us is to find a criterion
that permits us to identify the narrator.

Conversation often progresses by dialogues, evoking
mostly conversations of years ago. Sometimes we know who
repeats them, and perhaps even to whom. If the dialogue
is accompanied by comment, the function of the narrator
resembles that of the chorus of antiquity or the narrator in the modern theatre. Often, however, nothing is
revealed to identify the narrator but for a few obscure
hints dropped chapters (or at least a good many episodes)
before.

Author and narrator are not identical if the fictitious narrator is placed on the level of the narrative,
whereas the author remains outside it.

It is not necessary for the narrator to relate his
thoughts in first-person singular: it is sufficient for
us to see the events through his eyes and with the assistance of his thoughts. If a third-person narrative
can be rewritten into a first-person one without any
difficulty or any special additional changes in the text,
then the person whom this first-person narrative fits
can be regarded as the narrator.

The novel consists of four books. Everything that
one reads in those four books is uttered, by the fiction
of the novel, by Ambrosio and Santiago, in a *cantina*
called La Catedral — or, if not actually uttered, that
is where it surfaces in their thoughts. All that they
actually say to one another is either preceded or followed by a present-tense *dice* ('he says'). The action
itself, on the other hand, is presented by the author in
the form either of conversations in the past, marked by
the past-tense *dijo* ('he said') or of flashbacks, in
which further narrators are introduced (with the single
exception of the first chapter in Book I). Just as
Ambrosio and Santiago, these further narrators, too, are
actor-narrators or even protagonist-narrators. In Chapters 2, 4, 6, 8 and 10 of Book I, Santiago is at centre-
-stage, and is also the only narrator, but for Chapter 2,
where his friend "Popeye" functions as co-narrator. In
principle, Chapters 3, 5, 7 and 9 should be narrated by
Ambrosio. He is, in fact, present in each: in Chapters
3 and 7 he talks of don Cayo and his underlings to a
certain "Master" (don Fermín), unnamed as yet. Chapter
9, on the other hand, is an evident sequel to Chapter 7,

but without the least hint at Ambrosio's role as a narrator. The real protagonist-narrator in Chapter 5 is Amalia; Ambrosio is present only in so far as the conversation in La Catedral also turns to Amalia, and the author weaves remarks made there into Amalia's relation.

In Chapter 3, beside Ambrosio, the Lieutenant, whom the then Minister of the Interior, Colonel Espina (the Serrano), has sent for don Cayo Bermúdez, picked out to be Head of the Security Service, is another narrator. Eventually, the story is taken up by don Cayo himself, who relates things that Ambrosio could not possibly have known about. The unique dialogue-labyrinth of Chapters 7 and 9 precludes the identification of any single narrator. In fact, Trifulcio tells his own story; Ludovico relates all that has to do with the interrogation of Trinidad, and from some scattered minor comments one infers that don Cayo may be the narrator of the dialogues between himself and the politicians on the one hand, and the henchmen of power on the other. Don Cayo as narrator invariably addresses himself. Ludovico's story is revealed in a conversation between Ambrosio and don Fermín, a conversation that predates by a long time Ambrosio's meeting with Santiago, son of Fermín, in La Catedral.

The narrators in Book II are don Cayo, Amalia, Santiago, and Ambrosio; those in Book III are don Cayo, Amalia and Santiago. In Book IV, don Cayo, who has fled the country meanwhile, is replaced by Queta. Santiago, Ambrosio and Amalia remain accessory narrators.

The above enumeration of the narrators is necessary as a preliminary to distinguishing the various events and story lines of the novel.

The novel begins under Odría's dictatorship. It partly tells about how power operates (securing for itself the support of the big landowners and big capital and of the army, and deploying police terror), and partly about the attitudes it prompts the individuals to take. The most prominent representative of this latter relation is Santiago, son of rich don Fermín. His political activity as an undergraduate comes to an abrupt end when his influential father springs him from prison where his friends are held captive. In his great shame, Santiago breaks off all contact with his friends and with his family as well. He becomes a journalist, partaking neither of power nor of money, but also giving up, at the same time, all intention of doing something to change the existing order. After his separation from his love (Aída) and his friend (Jacobo) and the movement, he experiences yet another shock when he learns that la Musa, mistress to don Cayo, ex-head of the Security Service, was most probably murdered by Ambrosio, don Fermín's (and don Cayo's) chauffeur, presumably because she was blackmailing don Fermín about his homosexual relationship with Ambrosio. The case is hushed up, and Santiago subsides into his uninteresting everyday life, relatively nice marriage and humdrum journalist's job.

Book I can be divided into three story lines: Line 1 encompasses Santiago's life from the time when he is preparing to sit for his university admission examination to his arrest in his third study year; Line 2 traces Amalia's life with Trinidad from the same year when Santiago is preparing for his exam and is interrupted by the death of Trinidad; Line 3, concerned with power,

pursues the acts of don Cayo, Head of the Security Service, the wielder of power, and presents the instrument
(Trifulcio) of that power and its victim (Trinidad, unnamed here, beaten to death on interrogation by Hipolito). This last line begins after October 1948, when
don Cayo is brought to Lima by the Minister of the Interior, that is, some three years earlier than the other
two.

In Book II, one of the story lines is a follow-up
on Santiago's life. Having left his family, he gets a
job at the daily paper *La Crónica* and makes friends with
the miscarried poet Carlitos. Line 2 is the story of a
single day in the life of don Cayo compiled in fact out
of the events of several years: it sheds light on his
political activities and on his perverse love life with
la Musa and Queta. Line 3 brings us to la Musa's life
and is interleaved with the revival of the love affair
between Amalia and Ambrosio, interrupted when Amalia was
still a maid at don Fermín's. Line 4 is actually attached
to the don Cayo story, with Ambrosio relating to don
Fermín the sort of jobs he and Ludovico had been doing
together, for example, forcing the people of a workers'
district to attend a political mass meeting, putting
down a revolt of women workers, etc. Within a single
chapter, each story line is carried on by three narrators at most.

In Book III, one of the story lines is about the
investigation of la Musa's murder, in the course of
which Santiago learns about his father's affair with
Ambrosio, the probable murderer. Chapters 2 and 4 pursue
the don Cayo line: the rolling up of the Espina conspiracy and Cayo's fall after the failure of his Arequipa
plot. Line 3 follows la Musa's life after don Cayo has

103

left the country; all this we learn about from Amalia, who gives birth to Ambrosio's daughter at the exact time when la Musa is killed.

In Book IV, the Santiago line relates his meeting Ana, whom he then marries, don Fermín's coronary thrombosis and death and the marriages of Santiago's brother Chispas and sister Teté. Line 2, a conversation between Queta and Ambrosio, sets forth how the two of them have met, and also Ambrosio's telling Queta about his affair with don Fermín. Line 3 is co-narrated by Amalia and Ambrosio. The short-lived happiness of their Pucallpa days founders in misery and ends in Amalia's death. Ambrosio wreaks a vengeance of sorts on the person who has ruined him and then returns to Lima.

Only those series of events and story lines can be considered independent narratives which begin in 1949 or 1951 (or 1952), and progress, albeit discontinuously, towards the present of the narration. There are at least three shifts of time among these; their interleaving presents opportunities of flashbacks to earlier instants of the narrative.

Books I and IV end with events that have taken place very shortly before the present of the narration, whereas the two middle books close with earlier events, directing the reader's attention back to the past.

Assuming that the story lasts from end-1948 to end-1966, only the strands about don Cayo and Trifulcio can be regarded as prehistory. The time frame is shifted, though, if the onset of each story is placed into the moment that the relevant personages are introduced into the novel. In this case, the early love of Amalia and Ambrosio at don Fermín's also becomes prehistory, and so perhaps does Ambrosio's conversation with Queta, since it

is only from Book II on that Amalia keeps the reader informed about Ambrosio more or less continuously. The beginning of their relationship can be regarded as a
shared prehistory, just as the first meeting between
Ambrosio and Queta can.

At the formal level, however, Ambrosio's prehistory
is non-existent, since the strand in question tapers off,
so to speak, in the flow of the narration, rather than
being developed in interpolated set pieces breaking its
continuity. Thus, formally at least, prehistory is integrated into the story itself. Yet we might just as
well say that the rotating-narrative technique transforms any past-in-the-present into prehistory.

The interpolated fragments of dialogue reach forward
or back to certain important events, and, occasionally,
the same episode is related by the author summarily or
in dialogues in several story lines. Thus, for instance,
three events turn up repeatedly: the death of Trinidad
(Amalia, I.5; don Cayo, I.9), don Cayo's fall (Amalia,
II.7, 8, 9; Santiago, II.7; don Cayo, III.4) and the
death of la Musa (Santiago, III.1; Amalia, III.3).

Before studying the interrelationship of the three
story lines in regard of their temporal sequence, we
have to identify the dates to which the various events
can be assigned.

*3) The events: chronological order and place in the
   narration*

To those unfamiliar with recent Peruvian history,
Vargas Llosa does little enough to date the various episodes. Only the historical events provide fixed dates:
Odría takes power on 27 October 1948; he is elected pre-

sident in July 1950; the Arequipa revolt takes place at end-1955; the election campaign in favour of Belaúnde is launched in 1961, and he is elected in July 1963. However, some important motifs of the novel fit hardly if at all into the frame defined by these historical events. That is the reason why, in the *Table*, the chronological order of the main events had to be presented in three alternatives (see pp. *101-6*.)

If, in 1950, Santiago was in the second year of grammar school, he could enter university in 1953; that is, he could be arrested, together with the members of the Cahuide group, at end-1955 only, whereas that year is famous for the Arequipa revolt and don Cayo's downfall. However, at the time of Santiago's arrest don Cayo is still Head of the Security Service: it is he who exposes the Espina conspiracy three months after Santiago has been arrested. And yet, the Landa-Fermín-Arévalo group evidently needed some time to bait the Arequipa trap.

La Musa was killed either in 1957 or 1958 on the contradictory evidence presented. This would mean that the novel ends in 1962 or 1964 at the latest, since Ambrosio says his daughter, whose birth coincided with the death of la Musa, to be five or six years old at the time of his conversation with Santiago at La Catedral. Santiago, on the other hand, avers to be past thirty at the time; that is, if he was fifteen in 1950 (i.e. exactly Vargas Llosa's age), then Santiago meets Ambrosio in 1966; and that is the time when the story ends and retelling begins. Nor should it be forgotten that Vargas Llosa began writing *Conversation in the Cathedral* in 1966. Two more data support this version: according to Carlitos, Santiago "ceased to live" at the age of 18 ("You, it would seem, you stopped living at 18"; p. 172), and, on seeing la Musa's murdered body, Santiago says in a soliloquy, "You've been dreaming of her for ten years, Zavalita" (p. 372).

If la Musa had died in 1958, 15 months should have elapsed between Prado's election and her arrest, and that seems much longer than the events recounted in Amalia's story.

Table
Chronological order of main events

Santiago is born in 1936	Santiago is a third-year under-graduate in 1954	In La Catedral Santiago is past 30; Ambrosio's daughter is 5 or 6
	End-1948: Odría comes to power[*] Trinidad is arrested for the first time	
	First half of 1949: Parades offers the Spanish equivalent of first-name terms (*tutearse*) to don Cayo Don Fermín tells don Cayo that Santiago is in his second grammar-school	

[*] Historical events are shown in italics.

year
Don Cayo has in-
stalled la Musa in
a love nest

Mid-1950: elections

1951: don Fermín of-
fends don Cayo
Santiago wants to
enter at San Marcos
University

1952: don Fermín offends don Cayo Santiago wants to enter at San Marcos University	1952: Santiago is a freshman Sept. 1952: Trinidad is arrested for the second time Amalia is four months pregnant
1953: Santiago is a freshman Trinidad is arrested Amalia is pregnant	1953: Trinidad is arrested for the third time; he dies Amalia's child deadborn
1954: Trinidad is arrested for the third time; he dies Amalia's child deadborn	1954: Santiago is arrested; he breaks with his friends and family and "dies"

1955: Santiago
"dies"

Early 1955: Expos-
ure of the Espina
conspiracy
End-1955: Arequipa:
Trifulcio dies, don
Cayo is defeated

1956: Prado is
elected president:
La Musa is released
from prison
Amalia is pregnant
again

1ST VERSION

1957: la Musa dies
Amalita is born
Amalia and Ambro-
sio go to Pucallpa
Nov. 1957: don
Fermín's coronary
thrombosis

1957: Santiago
"dies"
(If the story
ends in 1966,
and Amalita is
6 at the time,
then la Musa
must have died
in 1960, but
since Santiago
is 21 when la
Musa dies, he
must have been
18 in 1957, at
the time of his
"death".)

109

2ND VERSION
    1958: la Musa dies
    Amalita is born
    Amalia and Ambro-
    sio go to Pucallpa
    Don Fermín's cor-
    onary thrombosis

1ST VERSION
    1958: Santiago
    marries

1ST VERSION
    1959: Amalia dies
1ST VERSION
    1959: don Fermín
    dies (a year and
    a half after his
    coronary throm-
    bosis)
    Santiago marries

2ND VERSION   1ST VERSION
    1960: don Fermín   (if Amalita is 6
    dies   at the time of
    1960: Amalia dies   the conversation)
    (don Fermín dies   la Musa dies in
    two years after   1960
    Santiago's mar-   don Fermín's cor-
    riage)   onary thrombosis
1ST VERSION
    1960: don Fermín
    dies

      1961: don
Fermín dies
(if Santiago
marries at
end-1959 or
in early 1960)
Teté marries
in 1960
Febr. 1961:
Chrispas
marries
March 1961:
don Fermín
dies

2ND VERSION
      1961: la Musa
dies (Amalita is
5 at the time of
the conversation)
1961: don Fer-
mín's coronary
thrombosis

Second-half
1961 or first-
half 1962:
Belaúnde's
first pre-
election tour

1ST VERSION
Amalia dies in
1962

Teté's wedding
(in which case
Santiago would
marry in 1961
and don Fermín
would die in
1963)

1ST VERSION
Don Fermín dies
in 1962

Second-half	Amalia dies in
1962 or first-	1963
half 1963:	
Belaúnde's	
second pre-	
election tour	

Teté is pregnant	don Fermín dies
Chispas and San-	in 1963
tiago have their	
talk about their	(If don Fermín
father's fortune	died in 1963,
not before 1963,	Santiago's talk
because *in 1963*	with Chispas
Belaúnde has al-	occurs no later
ready been in-	than 1964.)
vested pre-	
sident	

112

By the diverse pointers given, the deaths of the
characters concentrate in either 1954, 1955, 1957, 1960,
1962 or 1963. The following events may have happened in
the same year: Trinidad's death and Santiago's quasi-
-death; don Cayo's fall, Trifulcio's death and Santiago's
quasi-death; the death of la Musa and the quasi-death of
Santiago; the deaths of la Musa, don Fermín, and Amalia;
and, in several versions, the deaths of Amalia and don
Fermín. Those concentrations which include Santiago's
quasi-death fall between 1954 and 1957, the two dates
that mark the most agonizing period of Santiago's life
history.

The main conflict of chronology is that if Santiago
is of the same age as Vargas Llosa, his arrest ought to
have occurred after don Cayo's downfall; but even beyond
that, the chronologies of the various stories are inconsistent not only between them, but also with the historical dates. As a result, there is hardly time enough
for a love affair to develop and to end between Amalia
and Ambrosio while the first still serves at don Fermín's;
even more obviously, the year and a half that, according to Santiago, passes between don Fermín's heart attack
and his death is untenable, considering that all the
other events he relates — his marriage, his break with
his family, the period of reconciliation, the marriages
of Teté and Chispas — are supposed to have occurred
during that span of time. This is all the more surprising since, in this section of the story, there is no
longer any reason for Vargas Llosa to get entangled in
all these chronological contradictions; yet those are
far too frequent to be considered simple mistakes on his
part.

In each of the four books each of the three story
lines is attached to two periods of time at least; one
of these covers as a rule events that had occurred a
good many years earlier. In Book II, one or two such
sequences of past events are embedded in the other story
lines. This also points to the fact that the chronicle
of events does not coincide with the chronology of the
narrative.

After Chapter 1, the statement of the frame-story,
there are three time reversals toward what is the past
as related to the dates of the individual chapters: from
end-1951 or -1952 (Chapter 2) to end-1948 (Chapter 3),
then back to end-1951 or -1952 and back again to 1949
(Chapter 7), forward to end-1954 or -1955 (Chapter 8)
and then back to the middle of 1950 (Chapter 9) and,
finally, back again to end-1954 or -1955 (Chapter 10).

Figure 1

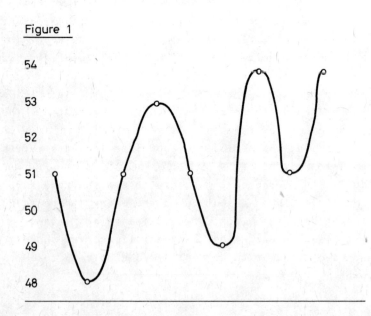

The most recent events occur in the closing chapter. This alternation can be represented in a system of co-ordinates as follows.

In the next two books the time displacement between the three story lines is still there, but all three end in events earlier than their own beginnings, that is, the story moves backward in time, in contrast to forward--moving Book I.

Book II places the stories of Amalia and Santiago in 1955; don Cayo's story dates rather vaguely to the second half of 1950 and to 1951 (including the events concerning Trifulcio and Trinidad). The narrative order of the three stories which alternate, in most cases three times within each chapter, can be represented as follows:

Figure 2

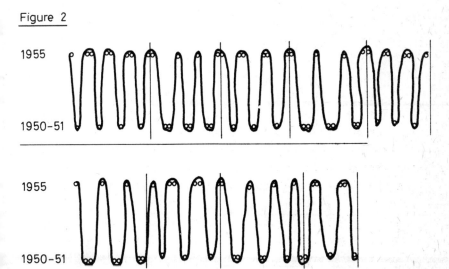

In book III, the year 1957 (or 1958) is followed by early 1955; then, after the events from end-1955 to mid-1957 or -1958, the narration returns to the year 1955.

Figure 3

1957 or 1958

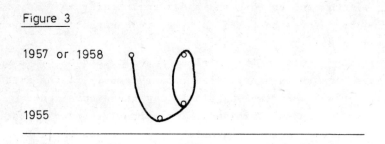

1955

The Queta line of the last book ends no later than 1963. Its dates alternate, within each chapter, with the events comprised between 1958 and 1963 or 1964 of the Santiago and Ambrosio-Amalia lines.

The last chapter returns again to the present of the frame-story. Queta's story ends some three years earlier. The triple rotation shows a downward tendency, just as in Book I: see Figure 4, Parts I and II.

The anti-clockwise rotation of the narrative of the two central books ends upon the don Cayo story, implying the "retrograde" quality of both power and public life.

The story lines relating individuals' (Santiago's, Amalia's, Ambrosio's) lives all move forward in time. The earlier episodes are more promising of favourable turns of event or of the characters' successful self-realization; where the narration comes closest to the

Figure 4. (Part I)

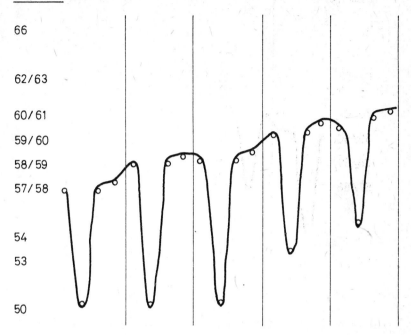

present, there stands the death of Amalia and the final
suffocation of Santiago's and Ambrosio's lives. (As to
character evolution, however, Ambrosio is a special case,
as we shall see later.)

4) Duration

The dialogue is that form of narration which, in
principle, lasts as long as the fragment of action it
relates. Since, however, one is a written text, while the
other is (imagined) speech, whose pace is subject to a

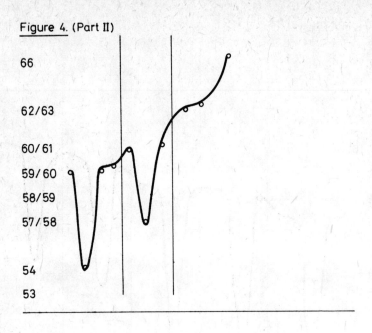

Figure 4. (Part II)

66

62/63

60/61

59/60

58/59

57/58

54

53

great many factors (emotional motivations, distance between the interlocutors, etc.); even this comparison of
durations of action and narration are closest. Indirect
speech lasts somewhat longer than direct speech, yet it
is the duration of a summary, for example, that is prac-
tically impossible to measure against the action it relates. Gérard Genette suggests that the spatial length
of the text (number of lines, pages, etc.) be compared
to the duration of the action.

An examination using this approach yields the following results[*] (see also *Fig. 5*): 135-odd pages of the

---

[*]   All data refer to the English edition of the text
(cf. Note 2) if not otherwise specified.

601 making up the novel cover relatively long periods
of time (ranging from one week to several years); these
sections relate in more or less detail the events taking
place between end-1948 and 1966 (or 1962, 1963 or 1964,
according to the other possible interpretations). Some
periods are only hinted at, while others are summarized
repeatedly. Thus, for example, Book I summarizes the
same year and a half from the points of view of Amalia
and Santiago, respectively, while Book IV gives a summary of the lives of Santiago and Ambrosio after the
death of don Fermín and Amalia, respectively.

The space of narrated time does not exceed eight and
a half or nine and a half years in all (to these, the
author devotes 133 pages) and the novel ends with another
short summary (10 pages) covering some five or six years
in the lives of Ambrosio and Santiago.

The above data reveal how markedly the pace of the
narration accelerates in the second half of the last
book.

Some 51 of the 188 pages of Book I relate the events
of slightly less than four years (within this period, a
certain calendar year and a half is covered twice). Another 36.5 pages give an account of Santiago's three
years at university, and 14.3 tell about Amalia's year
and a half. As for Santiago, only Book IV covers a relatively longer period of his life (on 19.5 pages).

In Book II, Amalia gives Gertrudis Lama an account,
on 3.2 pages, of her first affair with Ambrosio, the
exact duration of which is indefinite, but probably a
few months only. Then, in Book III, she relates the
events of the 18 (perhaps 32) months between don Cayo's
downfall and the death of la Musa on the one hand, and
the birth of Amalita and their departure for Pucallpa on

the other — on 26.4 pages in all. In Book IV, she and
Ambrosio relate on 20.5 pages the story of the slightly
more than two years they spent at Pucallpa.

Figure 5

No.	Length (pp) of book	Length of summary (pp)
I	188	51
II	135	3.2
III	133	26.4
IV	135	52

Accordingly, the proportion of the fast to the slow
sections of the narration is as follows (in round figures):

Figure 6

No. of Book	Fast:slow sections
I	1:4
II	1:42
III	1:5
IV	1:3

Virtually absent from Book II, the device of accelera-
tion is most notable at the end of the novel. Books I and
III are third and second, respectively, in diminishing
order.

In Book I, occasions of the same persons conversing recur twice or three times in one and the same chapter, and their several dialogues repeatedly touch upon the same subjects. These dialogues, even between the same pair of speakers, occur at different times, and if the reader gains the impression that they are continuous, that is just due to the writer's "dissolve" technique. This doubling and even tripling gives the narration a high frequency.

In Book II, repetition-based frequency is attained, first and foremost, by formal means. Within the same chapter, the author typically returns three times to the same story line.

The repetitious references to the Espina conspiracy and the events at Arequipa on the one hand, and don Cayo's downfall on the other, are not of a formal nature. The Espina conspiracy is suggested to don Cayo as a possibility already by Captain Paredes; Norvin informs Santiago of its exposure, and then Santiago's brother, Chispas, also alludes to it as an event that had shattered the finances of the family. Amalia first hears about the Arequipa revolt from Ludovico, and then from Carlota and the other maids and from Ambrosio. We learn from Amalia about la Musa's reactions to don Cayo's downfall and flight.

Chapters 2 and 4 of Book III, expounding both events in detail, further heighten a frequency that is high as it is. The action is carried along in both cases by the conversations of a great many persons. The ceaseless changing of both interlocutors and scenes contributes to raising the frequency pitch at the formal level also.

The only thing that can be regarded as a prehistory to Chapter 1 is the series of fragments addressed by don Fermín to Ambrosio, but at the time we read them we are still in complete ignorance as to the circumstances provoking his words and even of his, and the addressee's, identity. The lack of all previous information generates an effect of surprise. The reader cannot foresee that la Musa will be murdered; neither can he be aware of the identity and motives of her murderer — all these facts will endow don Fermín's comments with retrospective meaning, amplifying to the conscious level their earlier low-key, subliminal frequency. Chapter 3 contains certain antecedents to and aftershocks of a murder that was treated as an accomplished fact in the previous chapter. Its immediate antecedents and motives, however, are revealed in Book IV only, in the conversation between Queta and Ambrosio. Assuming that the significance of an event correlates with its frequency, the assassination of la Musa — surfacing as it does so often in the novel, even though mostly in the form of allusions only — obviously occupies a distinctive position within the narration.

In Book IV, no episodes or conversations recur. There are only repetitions of a formal kind, and these, too, are somewhat more emphatic in the first four chapters where Santiago narrates events twice in the same chapter, whereas, in the four closing chapters, even this low frequency tends to die down.

The summarizing narrative mode, on the other hand, is gaining ground. Only the Queta line is carried on in dialogues but, as it has been mentioned already, this is the only line referring back to la Musa's assassination and its antecedents. Thus, high frequency is, to a certain extent, a characteristic feature of Queta's narration as well. The importance of a certain event, situation or scene is increased by its high frequency, but frequency strength is not necessarily directly proportional to dramatic tension. As we have already seen, that is the reason why the author does not prepare the assassination of la Musa as directly as the Espina conspiracy or the Arequipa mutiny. The dramatic nature of the last two episodes is, to a great extent, the result of the dialogue form.

Dialogue, the specific form of the dramatic genre, has a great many functions in the novel. Apart from the second part of Book IV, Ambrosio relies almost exclusively on this form of narration. His lack of comments and the indifference and insensitivity revealed in those few that he makes, all contrary to the tension-generating potential expected of the dialogue, manage to degrade even the most shocking events to a humdrum everyday level. As a result, we come to regard the events retold by him as the all-pervasive features of Peruvian life rather than a string of isolated atrocities.

The summaries of Santiago and Amalia are good examples of the narrative modes being used contrarily to their inherent characteristics. The tension is, in fact, generated, in both cases, not by the story's summing up, but the interior transmission. This is achieved by the direct registration (following the expessions "he/she thought") of Amalia's and Santiago's trains of thought and, in Santiago's case, by pieces of direct and indirect speech and self-addressing concealed — by typographical means — in his summaries. A third-person utterance exposing an interior world of great emotional tension is similarly effective (cf. the description of the feelings and emotions of the dying Amalia).

The tension of a high-frequency episode grows higher, the more numerous the forms (dialogue, direct or indirect speech interleaved in a summary, self-addressing, summaries at a high emotional tension) the author uses to relate it.

Ambrosio's accounts-in-dialogue usually tend to relax the tension. The Queta—Ambrosio dialogues (Book IV), on the other hand, providing as they do the first insight into Ambrosio's emotions, are the more effective for that. Their impact is intensified by the fact that those emotions surface only on occasion. Inarticulate both intellectually and emotionally, Ambrosio requires the presence of an interlocutor to make him adopt an attitude, take a value judgment, make a confession. The author presents the most shattering and lasting experience of his past, his encounter with don Fermín and the hours they pass together at Ancón, interleaved with Ambrosio's self in the frame-story present. The high frequency of the Queta line — condensating as it does don Fermín's chance remarks in the first part of the novel, unintelligible at the time, the affair of Ambrosio and don Fermín and the assassination of la Musa, that is, all that has prompted Santiago to strike up the conversation with Ambrosio in the first place — lend a certain intensity to Ambrosio's statements, however low-key they are elsewhere.

Silence, standing mute, has always been an effective poetic device. At the interrogation, the non-reporting of Trinidad, who is described by Amalia as very talkative, has a most dramatic effect. His few words can only be guessed from the reactions of Ludovico and Hipolito, and even then they have no communicative value: he is raving in the delirium of utmost humiliation.

The frequency value of the Trinidad episode lags in no way behind that of don Cayo's defeat. It is surpassed only by the assassination of la Musa. The murders of Trinidad and la Musa suggest that life in Peru stands in the sign of violence. The death of la Musa extends the compass of this statement to human life in general. This in fact is the probable reason for its higher narrative frequency.

The originator of the conversation, Santiago, is the knight-in-reverse of the Grail legend who starts to quiz himself and the world concerning the whereabouts of the Holy Grail *after* his adventures are over. After the high-frequency phase of his life, between the ages of fifteen and eighteen, and retaining that frequency, at least formally, for another three years, he is made, in Chapter 1 of Book III, the climax of the novel, the narrator of another high-frequency story by repeated questioning connected with the homicide investigation, its extension to his father, and his conversations with Carlitos. In Book IV, however, the frequency of both his and Ambrosio's narration dies down, to become quasi-linear like the cardiogram of a dying heart.

6) Ellipsis, a constant of discourse (5)

The main hiatus coincides with the event that is the most consistently and also the most intriguingly prepared: the assassination of la Musa. Its effects, like those of any fortunate artistic solution, are multifarious. It saves the novel from sinking, if only for a single scene, to a cheap thriller, while managing to capitalize on the tension generated by the mystery genre, so as to assure the dramatic character of this section, promoted by its dialogue-form. It is evident from the analysis so far that the narration is fragmented far beyond the hiatuses resulting from the omission of *res gestae* irrelevant for the denouement, the necessary concomitants of any longer-winded epic form. The writer camouflages this fragmentation by leaving dates obscure, effacing thereby the ellipses in the action to all intents and purposes. For the same reason, he often makes events separated by several years appear simultaneous. His recourse to the ellipsis is both voluntary and forced. It is forced in that the writer's intent is a complete panorama of Peru, unfeasible almost by definition. In order to create the illusion of completeness, he papers over the inevitable hiatuses by blending the scattered fragments into one continuous narration. Even the dialogues are interwoven: A's question is formally answered not by his interlocutor B but by C, the participant of another dialogue, whose words seem to take up A's story. This method, however, also fragments the dialogue, creating voids between the interlocutors.

In Vargas Llosa's novel, the two contradictory tendencies, i.e. elliptic speech and the apparent effacement of the ellipsis, create a certain narrative mechanism, just as the system of symbols in Gabriel García Márquez' *Cien años de soledad*, the characters in Onetti's *El Astillero* or the weather in Rulfo's *Pedro Páramo*.

Most present-day Latin American novelists use their persons, plots and situations as vehicles of their personal views. Not so Vargas Llosa. In his works, experience comes through unadulterated although, of course, not unorganized; as a stream of communication rather than as a string of symbols. His outlook is not revealed by the various elements of his novel — it is not these that we have to interpret, and neither do we have to delve down to the meta-story behind the story itself; if we wish to go beyond the situation report opening up on the first reading in the hope of reaching another reading that will bring us close to the author concealed behind his narrators and dialogues, we have to study the specifics of the discourse.

In Vargas Llosa's case, the second reading is borne by the technical objectivization of the discourse, rather unusual, especially to this degree, in the practice of his Latin American contemporaries. His stumbling dialogues reflect a broken world, a disintegrated human community; his recursive and tangled story lines replicate a society and its individuals endlessly straining at the same shackles; his contradictory chronology allowing of three different interpretations, projects his vision of the world as a labyrinth. In his quest for the order of the events, the reader is bound to walk and walk again the paths of his heroes, following this or that road sign, just to fetch up, at the end, against another artfully disguised wall of the labyrinth.

There is no single exact date within this universe of concrete facts, this force field surrounded by dates familiar from recent history; time serves as a means of deception, of will-o'-the-wisp, ungraspable irreality.

The inserted flashbacks and flash-forwards, the "anachronisms" (6) admit of no categorization. The technique of rotating discourse transforms the past into the future and the future into the past; it makes concrete situation reports seem timeless comments, "achro-

nies" (cf. Amalia's reflections on la Musa's house and
her life, etc.), and transforms what are really timeless
comments into story motifs (cf. Santiago's destiny-shap-
ing comments on himself and on the conflict situation he
is in). The process of the discourse is related to time
in curious ways, not only because it takes place in time,
also because its sequence is to be measured against the
chronology of events. If, therefore, an author attributes
as great a significance to discourse as Vargas Llosa
does, his attempts to dismantle the time dimension are
to be judged absurd, or at least paradoxical. The fashion
of the absurd, so widespread in our century, can
be traced back to one of the categorical imperatives of
philosophical thought: the philosopher places the subject to be examined into an absurd situation, so as to
make its specifics stand out in greater contrast while
the accidentals generated by its environment fade away.

In the story, the violence is generated by Odría's
dictatorship; on the level of the discourse, however, the
topical issues of the given political situation are relegated into the background and lose definition; unreal
time makes violence stand out in a naked reality of its own.

7) Character-tripling

Vargas Llosa integrates don Cayo's stream of consciousness into the objective, real environment. It would
be impossible and also superfluous to find a partner to
size up and evaluate don Cayo, for he alone knows himself perfectly: his inner world is built around unequivocal sexuality, and it is this single-mindedness that
makes him a personality without conflicts. Queta and

128

Amalia are similarly identical with themselves, but with
the latter at a much lower level of consciousness. Being
oneself, of course, is no moral worth in itself: don
Cayo is the most immoral person of the novel, and Amalia
is probably the most profoundly moral one, if by moral
we mean the quality of one's relationship to one's
fellow beings.

Caught in the vise of conflict, Santiago indirectly
re-experiences his father's agonies. Don Fermín struggles
between his sexual proclivities and a moral imperative;
each of his visits to Ancón shatters his image of himself. He is a stickler for purity, just as his son is;
all that Santiago does, in the final reckoning, is to
chase after the ideal purity of total self-consistency in
public attitudes — that is why he is so thunderstruck
at Jacobo's weakness in the face of the strike decision. ("I thought only the cell and revolution existed
for him — said Santiago —, and then suddenly there are
the lies, Carlitos. He too, is just flesh and bones,
like you or me" /p. 229/.) The key to his crisis is that
he cannot make up his mind to join the party, but cannot,
either, stop blaming himself for having backed out.

The motif of the son following in the footsteps of
his father occurs twice more. The Vulture is as hard-
-boiled, ruthless and cruel as his son, don Cayo. And
Ambrosio is almost as incapable of grasping what is
going on around him as his father, Trifulcio. They are
both predestined to be the catspaws of others, and this
is not in the least altered by the fact that the one is
a criminal, while the other had merely been battered
into weakness by his mother. Ambrosio, after all, repeats, at least in appearance, the deed of his father,
who had been condemned to prison for rape and murder,

when he creates the impression as if la Musa had been killed for sexual motives. Neither can we be certain that Ambrosio's act was not motivated in the least by sexual desire.

Certain features of character and destiny of the fathers and sons are thrice repeated in the novel. Those who do not suffer from conflicts are also three; and so are the conflict-ridden ones, the third beside don Fermín and Santiago being Carlitos, caught between his journalist's job and his frustrated poetic aspirations.

> You can get in, but can't get out; it is like a quicksand — said Carlitos, as if he were withdrawing or falling asleep. — You just sink in deeper and deeper. You hate it, but you can't escape. You hate it, but all at once you would do just about anything for a scoop. (p. 265)

And we may, perhaps, add the trio of those who understand nothing of what is going on, who are good only to be used by others: Ambrosio, Trifulcio and Hipólito. Despite their widely different intentions, they typically resort to violence, a violence that is not their "official duty" but stems from personal motives.

8) Distance between narrator and story

If we accept the proposition that, being the vehicle of less detailed information, a summary presupposes a greater distance between the narrator and the subject of his narrative than a dialogue, it is evident that, in *Conversation in the Cathedral*, this distance changes continuously as the discourse proceeds. The deeper the involvement of the narrator and the more important he

deems a certain period of his life to be, the greater
his distance from the narrated period; and, conversely,
the more indifferent the narrator is to the subject matter of his narrative, the closer he is to it; let us recall as an example Ambrosio's stories, related practi-
cally invariably in dialogue form, and the summary which
he gives at the end of the novel, when he speaks of himself for the first time as consciously as becomes a relatively autonomous personality.

In the dialogue that relates what had happened between Ambrosio and don Fermín, the narrator is Queta:
the reader sees the events through her eyes, i.e. those
of a narrator who stands, once again, outside the action
itself. However, because of the dialogue mode used for
the narration, the distance is by our assumption smallest
between Queta and the action.

Vargas Llosa makes the emotionally involved narrator
adopt a more or less emotionally flat demeanour by using
the summary form, the form that provides the greatest
distance; he almost makes him identify with the author-
narrator and chooses as the narrator of the dialogues,
i.e. of the smallest-distance form, someone whose more
or less neutral emotional attitude makes shift for the
objectivity provided by a greater distance. It is the
latent narrator of the dialogue who is farthest from the
omniscient, or potentially omniscient, author-narrator.

La scène dialoguisée directe devient alors un récit
médiatisé par le narrateur, et dans lequel les 'répli-
ques' des personnages se fondent et se condensent en
discours indirect. ... la notion même de *showing*,
comme celle d'imitation ou de représentation narrative ... est parfaitement illusoire ... Il ne peut
que la raconter de façon détaillée, précise, 'vi-

vante', et donner par la plus ou moins l'*illusion de mimésis* (pp. 184-185.)

Genette's above statement makes it clear that the novel as a genre increases the distance between the dialogue and the scene recalled, but Vargas Llosa deliberately creates the illusion of mimesis and of the smaller distance that goes with it.

The alternation of the different narrative modes and the consequent changes of the narrator-to-story distance result in a certain balance of objectivity which, however, is free of the effort of the author-narrator's distance-keeping; that is, Vargas Llosa does not deprive the reader of the gripping experience of direct presence and participation.

The various narrative modes cover longer life-phases and shorter events of quasi-instantaneous character, respectively. The information density of the latter is much higher of necessity. The practice of changing the narrative modes frequently within a chapter, and invariably between chapters, strikes a balance of sorts between the durations of the narrated events: the scanty information on the years approximately equals in aggregate volume the copious information on the hours.

As a result, however, the reader loses his sense of time, and thus the novel evolves no real time concept of its own. This corroborates our previous conclusion that time in this realistic novel is unreal and elusive.

9) Narratorial presence

Mimesis associates a maximum of information density with a minimum of narratorial presence. Vargas Llosa always picks one of the interlocutors in a dialogue as the narrator, although comments revealing his choice are few and far between. He manages thereby to combine the highest possible degree of narratorial presence with the greatest information density. This narrator, however, should by no means be identified with the author-narrator (even though no one in real life could reproduce a conversation of any length verbatim).

In the summary, a minimum of information density combines with a maximum of narratorial presence. The scantiness of information is either due to distance, or else to the fact that the narrator can only relate what he knows or remembers. Vargas Llosa uses several devices to supply those missing links which he judges necessary for the progress of the story. The most patent of these is when he replaces himself with Amalia. According to the frame story, all that Santiago learns about Amalia — her life with Trinidad, with Ambrosio or with la Musa should be divulged by Ambrosio. Yet however much Amalia may have told him, he cannot possibly possess her detailed knowledge of herself. Amalia is therefore retained as a second narrator. But there are situations which Amalia is in no position to relate (her feelings after her operation and just before her death); here, the author-narrator joins in, to blow up, to a maximum, in that sequence at least, the scanty information proffered.

Gérard Genette quotes the table of Cleanth Brooks and Robert Penn Warren about the different viewpoints prevailing in the narrative. (8)

Figure 7

	Events	
	analysed from within	observed from without
the narrator is a character present in the plot	the story is told by the hero	the hero's story is related by a witness
the narrator is not present in the plot as a character	the author relates the story as an analytic or omniscient narrator	the author relates the story as an onlooker

Genette reproaches the authors for confusing two issues: (1) Who is the narrator? and (2) Whose point of view prevails in the narrative? The first question is answered by the row; the second by the columns.

For "point of view" in the narrow sense, he proposes the term *focus*; in his view, there are three sub-types of focus

zero focus in the classical narrative;

inner focus: the story is told from the point of

view of a single character (but may be taken up by a second, a third, etc.);

   outer focus: the story is restricted to explicit phenomena observable also by outsiders (9).

If it is the narrator who sees, hears and feels, he always tells the story from his own point of view (except for the writer-narrator). However, it is not necessary for his narrative to have an *inner focus*. Ambrosio's narrative, for example, reproduces previous dialogues more often than not; he colours these with few comments if any; that is, he does not assert a point of view of his own.

It is reasonable to examine, for each and every narrator, whether he/she is present in his/her narrative, and how he/she asserts (or fails to assert) his/her special point of view. In *Conversation in the Cathedral*, the author-narrator does not figure as a character in the story. He takes up the narration only when the narrator's knowledge of certain details (most often of public events) proves inadequate (*zero focus*).

The frame story identifies Ambrosio and Santiago as protagonist-narrators. However, in the story proper they are not the only ones to play this role.

Ambrosio is often relegated into the background of a given event, even if he experienced it himself. In his account of don Cayo's youth, the central place is occupied by don Cayo himself; Ambrosio is just a supporting character. Elsewhere, he may have the same stature in the story as the other protagonists, for instance in his "jobs" with Ludovico and Hipólito. Some other events that he relates did not concern him at all; he is just repeating hearsay. Finally, in the last book, he is at the centre of his own narration.

The narrator Ambrosio may thus be a protagonist, a supporting character or a witness. Apart from the first case, his narration is mostly exterior rather than interior; that is, he does not assert a point of view of his own. But perhaps it is exactly this lack of a slant that is characteristic: from his low level of consciousness he cannot see behind the events. Therefore, his own image is reflected to some extent by the images he forms (or, in Ambrosio's case, often fails to form) of others. This tallies with Jean Pouillon's words quoted by Genette

...le personnage est vu 'non dans son intériorité, car il faudrait que nous en sortions alors que nous y absorbons, mais dans l'image qu'il se fait des autres, en quelque sorte en transparence dans cette image.' (p. 209.)

Although, owing to his low level of consciousness, Ambrosio has a rather narrow-angled vision of things even when telling his own story, it is nevertheless justified to speak of an inner focus in his case.

Santiago is, in most cases, the protagonist or co-protagonist of his own narrative. In the dialogues, his presence as a narrator becomes more low-key, but he does not fade out altogether. As he grows more indifferent and drifts away from his family and, simultaneously, from his youthful, struggling and conflict-bound ego, he backs increasingly into the position of a witness (cf. the death of don Fermín and the marriages of his sister and brother); at least this is what both the action and the low emotional key suggest, although, on the formal level, he remains the hero of his own narrative, the *focus* of which is clearly inner. Our image of him — which is, of course, not a perfectly authentic one — is based directly upon his self-examinations in the monologues. According to Genette, the internal monologue is the only form that allows a total *inner focus*

La focalisation interne n'est pleinement réalisée que dans le récit en 'monologue intérieur'... (pp. 209-210.)

The same is true for Amalia as well, although, at a much lower degree of consciousness, her interior monologue is rather of an emotional character (cf. her agony). She, too, is now the protagonist, now a supporting character or only a witness in her own narrative (as, for instance, in the sections about la Musa's life). Her presence as a narrator is always evident; of all the narrators, her point of view is the most consistent.

The don Cayo *line* mostly takes the form of dialogues, spiced with the occasional comment on the ways and means of holding on to power. The fact that the author usurps the narrator's role fairly often and that the narration then tends to *zero focus* lends these parts a certain objectivity. Whenever Cayo is the protagonist-narrator of his own personal life, his presence as a narrator is very strong.

The Cayo *line* has many narrators; its events are related by (or from the viewpoints of) several characters. Focus-changing, a characteristic device of the whole novel, is particularly conspicuous in these parts. Beside Trifulcio and Ludovico — and Ambrosio, who occasionally doubles in their roles — the author-narrator also takes up the thread of the story fairly often.

Trifulcio-Ludovico and Ambrosio are protagonists, supporting characters and witnesses, alternatively. Their presence is evident in each case. The sharpness of *inner focus* changes as a function of their levels of consci-

ousness, emotional saturation or indifference, while in
the dialogues, it tends to be replaced by an *outer focus*. In Book IV, Queta, the narrator, is sometimes a
supporting character, but mostly a witness only. The
first of her roles is characterized by *inner*, the second
by *outer focus*.

For the narrative as a whole, the *focus* of the dialogues — the dialogue being the dramatic form *par excellence* — is mostly *zero focus*: they seem to be narrated
by the author. However, they may also be seen as narratives with an *outer focus*, since they are limited to the
reproduction of what is experienced or heard.

The rich variations of both the narrator's attitude
to the story and of the points of view correspond to the
ternary principle of construction based on repetition,
as opposed to the one based on the simple contrast of
two elements. The essence of this approach is that three,
being more than two, is the equivalent of "many", "mani-
fold". Polymodality, discovered by Genette in the oeuvre
of Proust, is evidently a characteristic feature of *Conversation in the Cathedral* as well.

11) *The instant that triggers the narration; the duration of the narration*

The present of the frame story is to be considered
the present of the narration. Although its dating is ambiguous by the writer's intent, the possible alternatives
are confined to certain well-defined years. The present
tense "he says" (*dice*) always refers to the conversation
of Santiago and Ambrosio in La Catedral.

Genette classifies the time relation of story to
narration as follows

ulterior narrative (narration ultérieure)	traditional; the story precedes the narration
simultaneous narrative (narration simultanée)	story and narration are completely or nearly simultaneous
interpolated narrative (narration intercalée)	the narration is inter-layered with the story
anterior narrative (narration antérieure)	the narration precedes the story (the story-teller proposes, fore-tells, dreams about the action, etc.)

(pp. 229-231)

The last of these four variants is not typical of *Conversation in the Cathedral*, where such predictive utterances as occur are a result of chronology reversal, and can by no means be considered separate narratives in themselves.

Interpolated narrations (digressions), on the other hand, are fairly frequent, such as don Cayo's prehistory, or Amalia's and Ambrosio's affair at don Fermín's house, etc. But there are also several narrative levels inserted between the present of the narration (i.e. that of the frame story) and the relative past; it is through these that the story is told. These digressions cannot be dated even alternatively; the only thing known for cer-tain is that they occur not after the events of the nov-el, but in between them.

As for the simultaneous narration, Genette makes a distinction between variations based on behaviour on the one hand, and on inner emotional awareness on the other. In the first, he says,

> ... la dernière trace d'énonciation ... disparaît dans une transparence totale du récit, qui achève de s'effacer au profit de l'histoire ... (p. 231.)

whereas

> .. si l'accent porte sur la narration elle-même, comme dans les récits en 'monologue intérieur', la coincidence joue en faveur du discours et c'est alors l'action qui semble se réduire à l'état de simple prétexte, et finalement s'abolir ... Tout se passe donc comme si l'emploi du présent, en rapprochant les instances [the instances of the story and the narrative, that is], avait pour effet de rompre leur équilibre et de permettre à l'ensemble du récit, selon le plus léger déplacement d'action, de basculer soit du côté de l'histoire, soit du côté de la narration, c'est-à-dire du discours ...
> (pp. 231.)

The flow of narrative is initiated not only by the instant when in Santiago there surges the agonizing question of how he and Peru have become "screwed up"; the things that happened to the other narrators also trigger narrations. The narration as a whole is generated by the statement of existence as a problem, and this reacts, indirectly, upon each narration-triggering instant: existence compels the multiple narrative. The wish to "be in the picture", to understand what is going on, is inherent even in beings of such lowly consciousness as Ambrosio.

The interposed narratives may either antedate or post-date the general stream of the story, but they are mostly simultaneous or quasi-simultaneous relative to their own subject matter (as cf. Amalia's account of la Musa). These interposed narratives function as stories in the frame story; they are integral parts of the overall narrative. Consequently, they are of an active nature (action correlates). That is, under the overall narrative, the interposed narratives are transformed into actions, and this, together with the deployment of the narrators, demonstrates the unsatisfactoriness of the overall *narrative* itself.

Thus the interposed narratives confront the narration as action with the story as action. Nothing could be more justified in a work that resolves the hopelessness of social relations, and the relations between individuals among them, in the creation of creative narration.

The greater the time gap between the narration and the story, the more the actuality of the latter decreases. It can, of course, be restored at will by infusing the narration with a high emotional tension — of the "it is still aching" type — or, not necessarily in contradiction therewith, by showing the consequences of a past event that still matter, that determine the present to a certain extent. This is the relevance of Santiago's meditation on his "screwed-up" life to the narrative as a whole. The interposed narratives, on the other hand, tend to be close in time to, albeit not necessarily simultaneous with, the story. This shortens the distance so that events are experienced virtually at first hand. The time gap between the story and the narration is further narrowed by the fact that certain conflicting statements make the time covered by the story seem much shorter than it actually is. As a result, the instant initiating the narration also appears closer to the beginning of the narrated events. Ambrosio's and Santiago's conversation in La Catedral, if we take the former's words literally, may have taken place as early as 1962.

It would, however, be wrong to judge the interposed narrative only by whether they enhance the reader's impression of first-hand experience. They also have the contrary effect of not letting the reader forget, or at least of reminding him again and again, that he is listening to a narration. It is perhaps not beside the point to interpret the recurrent "he says" in the dialogues as warnings: the transmission is not "live" but a "playback". In fact, this technique at times emphasizes the discourse to the detriment of the *story*, and at times pushes the *narration* into the background *owing to* the immediacy of the story. Let us quote Genette again

> ... une des fictions de la narration littéraire, la plus puissante peut-être, parce qu'elle passe pour ainsi dire inaperçue, cst qu'il s'agit là d'un acte instantané, sans dimension temporelle. ... Contrairement à la narration simultanée ou intercalée, qui vit de sa durée et des relations entre cette durée et celle de l'histoire, la narration ultérieure vit de ce paradoxe, qu'elle possède à la fois une situation temporelle (par rapport à l'histoire passée) et une essence intemporelle, puisque sans durée propre.
> ... elle est extase, 'durée d'un éclair', miraculeuse syncope, 'minute affranchie de l'ordre du Temps'.
> (p. 234.)

Ambrosio and Santiago ostensibly recall the story of *Conversation in the Cathedral* in a few hours, but that, of course, is untenable fiction. The multiple narrative of *Conversation in the Cathedral*, and the instances triggering them as a succession of thunderclaps boost all that is meant by the instances and thus also the narrator's or the narrators' wish to break out of the relations defined by real time, and also their efforts to realize this wish.

Above we have pointed repeatedly to Vargas Llosa's deliberate attempts to deprive time of its reality. The interposed narratives are sufficient proof in themselves of his persistent destruction of time — not so much time in the abstract as the very real time that has passed during these eighteen-odd years of his life. He mixes up real order, shortens durations and negates the reality of the stream of time.

In this labyrinth of Chronos, our only guiding lights are the instants that trigger the narratives. With their help, we can cast off the shackles time puts on action and attain the narrator's present. There is, however, no progress in this present. The conversation in La Catedral is indivisible; it contains no before or after; it is to all intents and purposes condensed to an instant. The conversation does not create a new situation: after it, Ambrosio will be the same outcast Lima bum as before; nor will Santiago's life change. That is, narration brings no real release to the protagonist-narrators. The instant initiating the writing of the novel liberates the author-narrator only. The instants triggering the narration and the writing are not identical, but they are overlapping. Santiago may step out of his era, to state his existence as a problem in the narration; yet it is not he himself but the writer who is saved by the miraculous missed heartbeat, the *"minute affranchie de l'ordre*

du Temps". Only he, the creative artist, can re-experi-
ence this ecstasy in the present of creation with its
promise of a permanently self-renewing future.

12) *Levels of narrative -- narrators and "narrataires"* (10)

Vargas Llosa has repeatedly emphasized the great
value that he attributes to "nesting", the novel modelled
on the so-called "Chinese box". The outermost "box" is
the first chapter which encompasses all four books: the
remaining nine chapters of Book I, the nine chapters of
Book II, and the twelve chapters altogether of Books III
and IV. The frame story (Chapter 1) is followed by 30
other chapters (one each for Santiago's 30 years; this
number is a multiple of 3, as are the 18 years of the
action). Each level of the narrative corresponds to a
nested Chinese box.

Both the author-narrator and his audience (the
narrataire, the addressee, the reader) remain outside
the story. The novel has/may have several narrators and
listeners at the different levels of narrative.

The first level is the frame story with Santiago as
its narrator. Before his meeting with Ambrosio, he is
his own *narrataire* as well: he addresses the question
starting off his narration to himself. After their meeting, Ambrosio shares the role of listener and also that
of first-level narrator; as the latter, he has Santiago
as his *narrataire*.

They both function as (second-level) narrators *within*
the story as well. At the second level, Carlitos and don

Fermín respectively are Santiago's and Ambrosio's *narrataires*.

Amalia, don Cayo, Trifulcio and Queta are further second-level narrators, while Ludovico is a third-level one. The frame story suggests that, with the exception of don Cayo and Queta, the narrators' stories are all related by Ambrosio to Santiago. This type of indirect, transmitted narration interposes a virtual listener between the narrator and the reader, increasing the latter's distance thereby. In principle, it should make it harder for the reader to identify with the narrator. This distance, however, is lessened by the unspecified identities of the virtual *narrataires*, their unobtrusive presence, or the "condensation" of narrator and *narrataire* into one and the same person (as is the case with don Cayo, where the reader gets the impression that he himself is the listener); this sets up a more direct contact with the narrator with whom the reader can thus identify himself quite readily.

Two conflicting tendencies emerge simultaneously: the author keeps the reader at a certain distance from the narrators, assuring thereby that the latter observes the events objectively, from the outside, while the uncertain identity of the *narrataire* or the possible absence of one makes it easier for him to identify with the *narrataire* and, through him, with the narrator as well. In certain cases, as indicated already, the author unobtrusively takes over, making the reader sharing a level with himself, his listener.

On the other hand, although his presence increases the distance between the reader and the narrator, the *narrataire* may enhance the reader's receptive process by expressing opinions, making comments and asserting a

point of view of his own; he may provoke a self-questioning internal debate in the reader, and may force him
to mull over the novel, that is, to reassess his own
life.

x x x

All the points studied above go to prove that it is
the discourse of *Conversation in the Cathedral* from
which a second/third reading may emerge.

The narrators' identities have helped us to find our
way in the labyrinth of the narrative, to identify its
various levels. We may speak of first-, second- and
third-level narrators and listeners (*narrataires*) attached to the first, second and third level of the discourse.

We have tried to narrow down the dating of the narrated events, and have come to the conclusion that, with
the author deliberately contradicting himself, no unam-
biguous chronology can be established. Following his
guidance, we are liable to bump into walls, get into
blind alleys and wander about in a labyrinth. This labyrinth symbolizes Peruvian society, and suggests that, in
that society, time as historized by real-life dates
tends to be unreal. However, because of the nature of
the action, the unreality of time is no negation of
earthly existence, nor the assertion of an unearthly or
subjective reality. By painting an unreal time, Vargas
Llosa negates the actual social formation only, implying
its lack of reality, or, not to put too fine an edge on
it, its lack of authenticity. This further intensifies
our feeling that there is no way out of this particular
labyrinth.

The alternation of events predating and postdating the present of the plot, that is, the arrangement of the story lines, creates a temporal rotation. By the chapters or chapter fragments about power and public life at earlier dates, the narration goes back in time, implying the retrograde character of the events in question.

The events of private life gradually approach the present of the frame story. However, there is no progressive development in this respect, either, since the chances of or hopes for lucky breaks or fortunate choices decrease in direct proportion as time proceeds.

The above relationship between public and private life warrants the conclusion that, in a retrograde society, the life of the individual tends to be impoverished rather than enriched; that is, time plays a negative role. Earlier social events are followed by individual events more recent by a few years, implying a direct causal relationship between the social circumstances and the lives of the characters.

The high frequency resulting from the repetition of certain story elements, enriched by flashforwards and flashbacks, the references to a certain event or situation in several conversations and the recurrent surfacings of the different story lines all focus our special attention on certain key episodes: the boys' attempt to seduce Amalia, the torture of Trinidad, the Espina conspiracy and the bloody events of Arequipa on the one hand, and don Cayo's downfall, the affair of Ambrosio and Fermín and the assassination of la Musa, on the other. All these events are associated with violence. Their high frequency draws together these events scattered in time, and transforms the novel into a single sequence of violence-saturated vibrations. The episodes mentioned above all turn up in several of the stories. Only those experienced by Santiago remain within the bounds of the Santiago line. Is it, then, justified to speak of high frequency in connection with any of the episodes of Santiago's life?

To answer this question, let us choose for our point of departure that of the narrative: where did Santiago ruin his life and what has caused the ruin of Peru? The short ascending period of Santigo's life — coming to an end already in Book I — is the antecedent to the question posed by the frame story. This is all the more evident since, in Book II, the Santiago line contains insignificant events only, and the conversation between Carlitos and Santiago reaches its climax with the discussion of the original issue starting off the whole narration. All the high-frequency episodes enumerated above beg the same question, since "screwed-up" Peruvian public life is as much the cause of Santiago's foundering in grey monotony and hopeless despair as of the behaviour of those around him. The author's objective being to project the story as a whole upon the key question asked in the frame story, rather than to emphasize a certain action or situation, there is no reason for him to multi- plicate this or that episode of Santiago's life. There- fore, the changing frequency of the various books and events is consistently high with respect not so much to the various phases of Santiago's life, but rather to its meaning and quality.

The high-frequency episodes listed above are all fairly short. If the fifteen to eighteen years covered by the story were to be represented by a line, these events would plot on it as smallish dots. These high- frequency peaks are always transmitted in the dialogues

direct, or by playbacks at least, even if they are mentioned in the summaries, as in the case of Amalia's narration. Accordingly, the speeded-up summaries are coun-
terbalanced and surpassed by far in quantity by slow-
moving direct speech (by speeded-up we mean that form
of expression whose length expressed in pages is the
least compared to the duration of the event related).
That is, high frequency is associated in the novel with
slow narration — reproduced dialogues taking up, in
principle at least, the same space of time as their
originals — that is, frequency and pace are inversely
proportional in this respect.

Book II contains as we have seen, the most significant events. The conspiracy and the Arequipa revolt are
but new items here; they acquire their real frequency
value in the "direct" transmission of Book III. Book II
is also the slowest of all. Its subject matter is life
becoming a trivial routine. With its short episodes, it
represents the monotonous, meaningless years. In the
novel, a slow pace invariably underscores the importance
of a given event. This is why the author considers the
imponderabilities of Book II decisive from the point of
view of the general process. On the other hand, this is
why, in the last book, the author deprives the events of
their significance by decreasing the frequency and increasing the pace at the same time. That is, by the end,
Santiago has been through it all — his marriage, his
father's illness and death and the marriages of his
brother and sister — and no possible development can
affect him deeply or really change his fate. His great
fling, his spell of intensive life, is gone.

The author coordinates the pacing of the book with
the frame story (the last lines taking us back to La

Catedral), and the frame story, as we have seen, intones the whole story by an exposition of Santiago's first question. From Santiago's point of view, the Amalia—Ambrosio line is of little enough importance; that is why its low frequency is coupled with a fast pace. In Book IV, only the Queta line (largely made up of dialogues) is slow. However, it provides very important information on the affair between Ambrosio and don Fermín and the motives of la Musa's assassination. The narrative is slow-paced and its frequency is high if one considers the dialogue form and the content, but fast-paced in the events that it relates. Hence, this story line, too, fits into the general speeding-up throughout Book IV.

By the above, the summary is the narrative mode of the least intensity. However, our examination of the novel has shown that Vargas Llosa often uses the summary to express the introspection or emotional vibrations of his protagonist-narrator. In these cases, the rule that summaries are speeded up does not, of course, hold, since even dialogue takes much more time than timeless thought or perception.

The author uses the various narrative modes to characterize his heroes among other things. Most summaries inform us of the narrator's relatively high level of consciousness — or at least a richer-than-usual inner life, an emotional saturation and articulateness. Vargas Llosa often uses the dialogue — which usually expresses the interlocutors' relationship — as a vehicle of action, thereby moving his novel closer to the dramatic genre. His preference for point-like events (taking one day at most) over longer ones, i.e. his condensation of the action into crucial moments that would be easy to put on stage, is another drama-like feature.

Direct and indirect speech and the device of the summary all set up different distances between the narrator and the action. This distance should, in principle, be least in the direct transmission realized in the dialogue. However, whenever the narrator of the moment is most involved emotionally, Vargas Llosa prefers to use the summary even though, in principle, it projects the greatest distance.

Consequently, it is the protagonist-narrator, whose thoughts, too, are communicated and, consequently, he is the one who stands closest to the omniscient author-narrator and who contributes the most to the *narrataires'* identification with the author, despite his being sandwiched between the two.

The greatest distance between the narrator and the reader — where the author, not being a narrator, cannot address the reader directly — is lessened by that narrative mode of the greatest internal awareness, the summary, while the dialogue, where the protagonist-narrators disappear and the author-narrator, too, is impersonal, is deprived of its greater immediacy by its unemotional and action-oriented contents which constricts the reader's scope for identification.

In *Conversation in the Cathedral*, a minimum of information (as compared with the objective-time information flow of a given action) carries a maximum of subjective information, while the dialogue, rich in information, consistently represses the emotions trying to surface.

The *zero* or *outer focus* of the dialogue gives the reader the impression of obtaining untampered-with information. The summary, on the other hand, is seen to rely on inner focalization to a much greater degree.

Constantly changing the other features of discourse, too, Vargas Llosa does not maintain *inner* or *outer focus* throughout, nor does he restrict the presence of the narrator in the story to a single type; instead, he does his best to exploit all the possible variations, striving to offset the impression given by one type of *focus* by contrary effects generated by a different feature of the discourse or the content.

The duration of the narration as implied by the frame story is just a few hours. This duration is, of course, fictitious and, as such, impossible to measure or verify. The present of the narration — that is, one possible alternative chronology — is related to a year when both the protagonist-narrator Santiago and the author pass the age of 30.

The fact that the instant initiating the fictional narration of the narrator in the fiction is a concrete point of time in Santiago's life is to be considered symbolical. Vargas Llosa makes time unreal within the story. The exact pinpointing of the instant that triggers the narration is, in the final reckoning, an affirmation of the reality of the creative process, in the face of the unreality of the world represented in the novel.

Thus, the only "real" level of *Conversation in the Cathedral* is that of the discourse; that is the level where the author addresses his *narrataire*, the reader. The reader, according to Proust, is reading himself rather than the author (that is, in the novel, he is reading himself), just as the author is writing himself.

Since the *narrataire* is missing or unidentified on many levels of the novel, his place is free for the reader to take. This is how the reader is projected at intervals into the story just as the author is whenever required by the communication. Many levels of this fictional reality intensify and illuminate from several angles the author's and the reader's self-questioning embedded in the discourse for the former and in the listening for the latter.

The discourse emphasizes with predilection the fictional, illusory and unreal nature of a story which actually meets all the criteria of realistic representation (cf. the various levels of the narration, the narrators, the inserted pieces of mimesis, the chronological conflict). That is how the writer compels the reader to look beyond the fiction and the story at what had provoked him to write it; to concentrate, while reading, on reading himself into the conflict that had provoked the narration in the first place.

Vargas Llosa encodes his world view just as Rulfo, Onetti or García Márquez do, with the difference that his material is not atmosphere, character-drawing or mythology, but the exceptionally rich discourse of his novel.

Notes

Mario Vargas Llosa

(*1*) Discourse is an equivalent of the French term *discours narrataire* as used by GENETTE (cf. Note 3).
(*2*) Mario Vargas LLOSA: *Conversation in the Cathedral* (Conversación en La Catedral). Transl. Gregory RABASSA. Harper and Row, New York, 1975. 601. p.
(*3*) Gérard GENETTE: *Figures III*. Éditions du Seuil, Paris, 1972. The numbers in brackets all refer to this edition.
(*4*) Cf. GENETTE, op. cit. 145-182., 183-224.
(*5*) Cf. GENETTE, op. cit. 128-129.
(*6*) Cf. GENETTE, op. cit. 119-121.
(*7*) Cf. GENETTE, op. cit. 206-223.
(*8*) Cf. GENETTE, op. cit. 206-208.
(*9*) Cf. GENETTE, op. cit. 204.
(*10*) Cf. GENETTE, op. cit. 227., 265-267.

*The philosophy of Bataille and the world image
of Julio Cortázar*

Julio Cortázar's novel, *62. A Model Kit* is about relations developed and in the process of development between the members of a circle of friends. All of them
suffer anguish in some form or another: Juan, Nicole and
Marrast are tormented by the anguish of unrequited love,
Helène by impenetrable solitude, and Austin and Nicole's
first intercourse is spoiled by their knowing that Celia's
first sexual encounter took place with Helène. A couple
of more or less jolly fellows also belong to the group:
Tell, Juan's girlfriend, the two Argentines, Polanco and
Calac, and the mentally handicapped Feuille Morte.

The factual events of the novel are intermingled with
trips into the "City". Fictitious space — the not-easily-
definable ideological-spiritual City — and fictitious
time — the inextricable tangle of the elements of the
action — make the denouement fictitious too. We cannot
consider the City the domain of illusion, for several
characters wander into it and see each other there. So
it must at least be bordering on reality. The characters
take the same trams, traverse the same streets, head for
the same hotel; in other words, the City cannot be the
scene of a personal conflict. The *paredro* (untranslat-

able; relation comes perhaps closest to it in meaning) cannot be identified by any member of the group, but is embodied now by the one, now by the other. As the City is represented (to qoute Cortázar's words) by the city in which the characters temporarily reside, so the essence of the *paredro* is represented now by one, now by the other member of the group.

Those elements of the City that can be interpreted symbolically would make a psychoanalytic reading possible, but the fact that almost all of the characters turn up in it indicates that they are there forced to confront something that neither their psychic condition, nor their individual, concrete problems can explain, at least not in this extent. Consequently the City, this territory bordering on reality but not unequivocally identical with reality is the scene of a universally valid human conflict, a conflict which is unresolvable and even impossible to be made evident in the social sphere. The universal conflict of human existence, independent of place and time, demands by its nature a philosophical mode of raising the problem. This is why we consider the analysis of the relation between *62...* and philosophy justified. The oeuvre of Cortázar is without a doubt founded upon the experience of the meaninglessness, the irrationality of existence, or at least on the frustration of all attempts to discover the meaning of existence. The intention to break with the traditional language of philosophy among philosophers responsive or attentive to the crisis of European civilization became apparent already in the last century. Karl Marx, who considered this crisis the product of the existing political-economic order, used the language of the relative sciences (or rather, the language most suited for these sciences) for the exposition of his ideas. Kierkegaard, true to his religious cast of mind, adopted the language of theology. To avoid the traps of both philosophy and theology, Nietzsche turned to the language of literature, and Wittgenstein's discussions of the language of philosophy led him to the conclusion that only silence is truly authentic. George Bataille takes the same standpoint in relation to the fundamental problem of our age: the distorted or impossible means of communication.

He, too, contests language, not primarily because of its present state, but because of its essentially discursive character, because of its design-orientedness ("Language is essentially, discounting its poetic distortion, design." (1) See the conversation of the circle of friends imitating linguistic patterns without using meaningful words. (2))

The fact that the action originates in a misinterpretable word is even more remarkable. The *chateau saignant* (an abbreviation of a Chateaubriand rare done) can be translated into Spanish in two ways: a bloody castle and a bleeding castle. The "bloody castle" evokes the atrocities of Erzsébet Báthory, and the brand of wine ordered by the protagonist (Sylvaner) the vampirism of the Transylvanian Dracula. This double association with reality is the consistent, determinative, basic metaphor of the novel.

> The result of the perversion of the language was ... something Juan couldn't name, because chain or coagulation were nothing but an attempt to give the level of language to something that represented itself like an instantaneous contradiction, took shape and fled simultaneously, and no longer entered lan-

guage spoken by anyone, not even that of an experienced interpreter like Juan. (3)

From the quotation it is evident that Cortázar, too, considered language unequal for the expression of certain experiences. Cortázar and Bataille's common standpoint concerning the validity of language would not in itself justify their comparison. But it does point out a significant fact: they both feel that the most valuable experience, the peculiarity of which is that it lasts but moments only, is inexpressible.

> But *beneath it all* I know that everything is false, that I'm already far away from that just happened to me... (4)

says Juan referring to his experience in the Polidor restaurant. However inexpressible one feels his inner experiences (*expérience intérieure*) to be, one cannot renounce imparting it to others. In Cortázar's novel we read that Juan was nevertheless

> Still persistent to revive that material which more and more was turning into language ... knowing that ... everything that he told would be falsified beyond repair, put in order... (5)

Bataille seeks direct and intensive contact with the world and with other people through inner experience. In this ecstatic (ex-static) moment man can forget himself and is able to reach the final limits of what is possible. In inner experience, words have no power, and man no longer asserts a right to be everything; he is content to be what he is,

> ... imperfect, unfinished, good to the point of being ruthless, clearsighted in his blindness, for he accepts the impossible, which is *per definitionem* inconceivable. (6)

According to Bataille

If I were to be allotted a place in the history of
thought it would be for perceiving in human life the
fading effects of that which is discursive reality,
and for having gained from the description of these
effects an evanescent light, a light that is perhaps
blinding, but one which signals the translucence of
the night, that signals, simply, the night. (7)

Cortázar, though indirectly, implies that the City
belongs to the realm of the night. Juan is surprised to
discover that Tell, this so very "diurnal" being — in his
opinion — has also been there.

In Bataille's night of inner experience it is the
famous night of the spirit that is reflected, the night
in which the mystic awaits his beloved. But Bataille
does not identify himself with the mystic who seeks to
gain salvation through losing himself. To seek salvation
is also a design, he says, and the only design he is
ready to accept is the one to end or break the design.
(The denial of language — language itself being design —
was conceived in the spirit of this break.) In his opinion, salvation is one of the most odious pretexts, for
the believer betrays that which originally determined
his standpoint: that the acquisition of experience is
impossible. Therefore, the only mystic he does not abhor
is the one who, in his yearning for salvation, goes so
far in his contempt of the design as to reject salvation itself, for salvation is also a design and may conceal some sort of ordinary, everyday interest. The rejection of the design, of knowledge, is the only guarantee
of disinterest. It is only through disinterestedness
that the perfect authentic moment may be achieved in inner experience. Bataille sees human dignity in the re-

fusal of every path that does not lead to the limits of
possibility, and makes everything questionable without
hoping for an answer.

It is hard to give a clear image of Bataille's ideas,
for he himself made no such attempt. His philosophy rejects thought and its medium, language, for his aim is
the imparting of the inexpressible. This is precisely
why he does not present his ideas to us in a logical
sequence, circling round the innermost core of his experience instead, approaching it from various angles. He
is intentionally inconsistent in his use of concepts.
The syntax of his philosophy resembles the circle closing in upon itself (the structure of *62...* is the same).
Any idea may begin and end any chain of thought. Because
of the interferences there is no possibility of a satis-
factory summation.

Bataille and Cortázar both strive to make their
existence authentic. For this they consider it indispensible to eliminate the conventions dictated by their
age. They both seek the gateway to that hidden but real
and existent realm in which man can shake off the fetters
of his own inner and external limitations and can establish direct contact with his fellow men and everything
that surrounds him.

This pursuit is apparent in most of Cortázar's writ-
ings, but apart from *62...*, the similarities between his
work and Bataille's philosophy do not transcend the
search for a more authentic reality. In *62...*, however,
not only the aim but also the means of realization coincide.

The function of the various planes of the novel is
to permit the characters to step outside their everyday
world and enter an ecstatic territory, which is trans-

cendental in the sense that it is *beyond* the boundaries
of everyday life, but is at the same time real, factual,
for it has nothing to do with the netherworld.

This transcendental territory is the real but at the
same time elusive City of *62*.... It is in this City that
the characters run their heads repeatedly against the
walls that separate them from other people, divide them
from a full and complete life.

In this City there is not a single building that is
a home: there are only markets, warehouses, hotels,
places that can serve as temporary abodes. Every building
contains a great many identical or similar items: the
market-place has its rows of stands, the warehouses its
rows of cans, the hangars their trams, and the hotels
their corridors and rooms. This multiplicity creates the
impression of inescapable repetition. We are wandering
in a maze of eternal identical elements. Cortázar himself uses the word maze

> What could have happened in the city had never wor-
> ried her as much as the feeling of following an itin-
> erary where her will had little bearing, as if the
> topography of the city, the maze of covered streets,
> hotels and streetcars, would always be resolved into
> a single, inevitable, passive course. (*8*)

The essence of the maze is that we may lose ourselves in it. According to Bataille we must step out of
ourselves in order that a true relationship may be created between ourselves and the other person through inner
experience. Those who lose themselves — who are lost —
have no home. The City is made up of motionless buildings and everything that moves in it: the trams, the
lifts, the pontoons seem to do so at their own pleasure.
The routes of the trams are not known; there are no call-

-buttons in the lifts, they glide up and down and horizontally without anyone working them. There is no defi-
nite schedule for the departure of the pontoons. Tell
calls the trams Nemesis. Trams, lifts and pontoons alike
are forces independent of man, the representatives of
fate.

In the City, the characters are forced to face up to
the evidence of their solitude — in the lifts for example,
or in the street of high pavements, where the gulf of
the street prevents contact between the two sides. In
their endless, aimless wandering they forget about themselves. Anguish is the force that urges them on. According to Bataille it is the not knowing, the irremediable
meaninglessness of life that awakens this feeling of
anguish. (9)

Anguish — he says — presupposes the desire of communication, the desire, in other word, to

... lose myself, but does not presuppose absolute
determination: anguish is at the same time proof of
the dread of communication, of losing myself. (10)

The wandering of the characters in the City displays the
same duality.

Hélène says to herself

My paredros ... would have said to me: We go to the
city but you only come, all you do is come from the
city... (11)

The Hélène who belongs to the City much more than any
other member of the group, who traverses the path to the
limits of the possible, is the one who strives most re-
solutely to steer clear of the City. And yet if she

... at that moment had wanted to be able to keep
every proof of the absurdity and the scandal forever,
to deny life its cotton and its compressess... (12)

that is, wanted to face the meaninglessness of existence, that may be ascribable to the fact that the meaningless death of the boy who died on the operating table forced her to question her conventional day-to-day life.

That is why she comes to the City as though she were leaving it, because she is more frightened than the others and because her fear moves her not only to question existence, but also to escape. Helène could as well pronounce Bataille's words

> I hate anguish, which a). tires me, b). burdens me with life, c). robs me of my innocence. Anguish is a guilty conscience. (*13*)

The always tired Helène, incapable of enthusiasm, incapable of relying on her feelings and instincts, is weighed down by a heavy burden in the City, a burden that is the symbol of her remorse. At the same time, she can only hope to lose her burden in the "ex-static" sphere of the City.

According to Bataille, inner experience is an independent, sovereign action in which thought is no longer a slave to familiar things but starts out from the unknown. To the sphere of this sovereign action belongs every type of effusion, everything we can experience in the way of eroticism, laughter, sacrifice and poetry. This effusion is achieved by laughter and by sacrifice through changing the order of things, like poetry does on the level of images. In *62...*, the poem about the City intercalated into the text is an excellent example of this method. No sooner has the action begun than the poem appears to embrace every element of the novel. It repeats more forcibly and in more detail the scene in the Polidor restaurant when the events to come (or have they already taken place?) suddenly become clear to Juan.

What is the City if it is not an image torn out of
the accustomed order of things, which is modified in its
every component: in its streets, buildings, public con-
veyances? The poem is not the only, simply the most obvious intrusion of poetry in the novel, a testimony of
an inner experience which the plot presents to us from
various aspects. The narrative is destined to represent
the indescribable. The experience transforms the immediacy of the inexpressible into language and at the same
time denies the efficacity of this, distorts the space-
time logics of the action. This is why the sequence of
events is irreparably upset. It is impossible to determine whether the Christmas Eve spent in the restaurant
precedes or follows the action.

The characters of *62...* participate in the sovereign
action of laughter rather than in anything else. It is
in laughter that the order of things is modified and it
is thus that the leap from the possible into the impossible is accomplished. The novel abounds in comic episodes, beginning with the snail race and ending with the
letter addressed to Neurotics Anonymous.

To discover the comic aspect of things, to submerge
in effusive laughter is a happy method of looking for
meaning where everything appears absurd, including the
one who is laughing. The explanation that man seeks in
vain concerning situations, phenomena, others and himself he believes to find in laughter, in this out-of-
joint and for this precise reason sovereign moment.
Laughter promises such dignity as can never be found in
everyday life.

The effusive peaks of eroticism appear in the novel
as a result of that avid desire to escape from an in-
sufferable situation. It is only while indulging in sex-

ual intercourse that the characters can forget themselves, do not feel anguished. On the night that Juan
spends with Helène they both feel that real, genuine
communication has been established between them. But
according to Bataille's interpretation, the sovereign
action, be it laughter, sexual intercourse or any other
type of effusion, can transport one to the brink of the
possible for moments only.

According to the philosopher, torment and suffering
can also transport one to the brink of the possible.
There are examples of this, too, in 62... Think of the
victims of Countess Báthory, and the references to vampirism, to the relation between the Countess, Frau Marta
and Helène intimated by the author. Juan sees two tiny
purple dots on the neck of the English girl, as though
Frau Marta had there sucked out her blood, and this scene
is directly followed by the one in which Helène places
her hand upon the sleeping Celia's throat. The basilisk
on the door of the house in Vienna reminds Juan of Erzsébet Báthory's house on the Blutgasse (Blood Street),
Helène's basilisk brooch, the victims of the Countess,
the dolls of Monsieur Ochs, and Frau Marta

> So that on that night the Viennese alleys led me to
> basilisks, which was the same as saying Helène, just
> as in the old, worn air that the stones of the door-
> ways seemed to exude, the Blutgasse was always pre-
> sent and then having remembered Monsieur Ochs was
> perhaps not so much a consequence of the basilisk
> house which had brought me to him, passing through
> Helène's brooch, but of the dolls, to the degree
> that the dolls were one of the signs of the countess
> who had lived on the Blutgasse, for all of Monsieur
> Ochs' dolls ended up tortured and torn ... in front

of the basilisk house all those signs were bringing
me back to the Countess. They brought her close, as
never before, to a region where fear vaguely throbbed,
and therefore when Tell had told me about Frau Marta
... it had been as if Frau Marta had come from before ... established and ordained by a meeting of
uncertain signs beneath the basilisk house ... around
the absence of Helène (*14*)

Helène is not responsible for the death of the sick
boy, yet in the City she nevertheless considers herself
his murderer; her sin and her remorse are authentic, for
she identified the boy with Juan, whom she denies her
love and thus robs of life. In sacrifice, the

... sacrificer is lost together with his victim, and
we see him defeated before an unfinished, unfinish-
able world. (*15*)

The sacrificer and the victim is fused in several
characters, especially in Nicole and sometimes in Helène.
As Nicole holds the sleeping Austin in her arms, she
imagines that she is making a confession to the *paredro*
(but it is perhaps the *paredro* who is imagining the confession) who says: Chalchiuhtotolin have mercy upon you,

the God of darkness, the eternal destroyer, whose
image is reflected only in the blood of sacrifices,
the precious water which is the blood of the torture
stone. (*16*)

Nicole, a victim of her unrequited love for Juan and
Marrast's unrequited love for her, protests that she is
not a victim

But I, father ... don't want to be a victim; I have
struck the first blow ... (*17*)

from which it follows that she recognizes the role of
her sacrificers. Cortázar compares Helène descending the

steps in the underground to Iphigenia walking towards the scene of her sacrifice. Helène, who sacrifices Juan and in a certain sense Celia, becomes the victim of Austin. Bataille sees the suffering of the victim as a possible source of ecstasy. It is in relation to this that he mentions the expression on the face of the Chinese prince subjected to torture during the Boxer rebellion: an expression that was a combination of suffering and ecstasy. Paroxysms of torment and ecstasy alike transport one to the brink of the possible.

Marrast

> ... between two dreams or vague murmurings from Nicole, who was asleep, I'd had a kind of vision of Helène tied to a tree and full of arrows: a miniature St. Sebastian... (18)

He thinks of the poem *Le martyre de Saint Sebastien* and the line that goes

> ... *j'ai trop d'amour sur les lèvres pour chanter*
> was coming back to me now with the image of Helène being put to torture, the council of the false gods, the time when Sebastian danced before Caesar ... in the dream I had glimpsed the image of Helène tied to the tree and not the profile of Nicole sleeping beside me ... Of course it was very easy to explain the figure. I'd thought of Helène as a substitute for Juan in order to erase Juan. (19)

> I'd gone back to sleep ... with the ironic notion that I was stealing images from Juan, because he was the one who should have been seeing Helène like that in his moments of insomnia, like that or in some other way, shot full of arrows or shooting them, but always cruel and unattainable, looking for a smile

... that appeared on her mouth at times to make our
lives restless with a rapid indifferent biting. (*20*)
Starting out from the fact that man is the only animal
conscious of death, Bataille points out that he is the
only one who can make death an impossibility. The tenor
of man's anguish is the impossible, and yet his anguish
drives him towards the impossible.

This is the reason for all the wandering in the City.
The purpose of the meeting to which Helène is hastening
is the reaching of the brink of the possible. When Tell
tells Juan that the high pavements led her to the edge
of the City, Juan says

Oh, the edge of the city, Juan said. Nobody knows
where it is, you know. (*21*)

In Bataille's opinion, to reach the brink of the
possible can only be accomplished through death. Helène's fingers release her burden only in the moment she
is stabbed to death, it is only in death that she is
delivered of the burden of her remorse. As Bataille says

No loss smaller than death is sufficient for the
radiance of life to permeate and transform pale and
dull existence, for only the free, uncheckable disruption of death can become the force of life and
time in man. It is only then that man becomes nothing
but the mirror of death, just as the universe is the
mirror of light. (*22*)

In the opening episode of the novel Juan sitting in
front of the mirror is made to face the maze of existence through the aid of the concurrence of elements aimed
at various forms of ecstasy. Juan becomes a mirror in
which ecstasy is reflected, the most perfect, most final
form of ecstasy being death.

Through the continual feedbacks time circles round from Christmas Eve in the Polidor restaurant to Helène's death. This is why any sequence of events is questionable. On Christmas Eve Juan already knows everything that is to happen, even Helène's death, though he relates this evening to his friends in the company of Helène. The novel ends with Feuille Morte's *bisbis*. If we think of the musical signification of *bis*, we may consider it a signal for repetition, which is not at all surprising in the case of Cortázar, who invites the reader to perform such repeated recommencements in *Rayuela*. But *bisbis* is also the meaningless manifestation of the mentally deficient Feuille Morte. In a work that opens with a linguistic ambiguity, our previous assumption is not unfounded — nor is the one according to which *bisbis* (in its end-stressed form) stands for a game of chance. This last interpretation is particularly tempting if we compare it with the role that fate or chance plays in Bataille's philosophy.

Besides the *per definitionem* active everyday reality and the passive inner experience of the City (which cannot be created by the individual), the novel runs on a third level: that of the imagination, a level on which the individual actively attempts to discover intimated, hidden reality. But hidden reality can only become manifest spontaneously — consequently the level of imagination is at the same time the level of frustration. The Oliveira of *Rayuela*, the Jimmy of *The Hunter* both strive desperately to discover this hidden reality. The sphere in which they search for the part, the gateway to the more authentic world never materializes and is strictly confined to the individual, to the imagination of the individual, unshareable with others.

The great novelty of *62...* is that the City is independent of the individual, it exists outside the individual as it were — for this reason is the scene of
common and universally valid experience — and is a territory which the characters do no enter of their own
free will. The City happens to them. Personality is a
passive agent of the inner experience materialized in
the City. To recall Helène's words,

> She was vaguely thinking about the city, where walk-
> ing always had something passive about it, because
> it was inevitable and all decided, fated... (*23*)

Meditative discourse

With the following analysis, we shall attempt to
determine the extent to which Cortázar's method coincides
with his world image, pervaded by Bataille's philosophy.

1) Who is the narrator?

All nine active speaking characters of the novel participate in the narration. Besides them there is a tenth
narrator we must account for: the mysterious *paredro*, who
can borrow the voice of each and any one of them, who can
be identified with all of them individually and collectively, and yet is not them, knows more than they do, and
yet does not dispense of a single fact that the characters are not aware of. He is not more omniscient than
they who constantly correspond with each other and are
thus fairly well-informed about the doings of the others.
(One must not forget that the customs of the group permit

every member to read any letter addressed to any one of them and because of this they are all familiar with each other's feelings.) The additional knowledge of the *paredro* is, therefore, not factual, but derives from the fact that he cannot be tied to any one character, yet exists concretely, though unascertainably by the reader in one or the other character; he speaks and sees simultaneously from within and without. He accepts the restrictions of the character but interfuses these with the freedom of the author.

The creation of the *paredro* and his role as a narrator bridges the gap between the author existing outside the narrative and the narrators of the novel. Through him Cortázar identifies himself with the collectivity of his narrator personae, with a sort of communal narrator who penetrates and permeates the characters, issues from them but surpasses them. As regards the frequency of occurrence, the *paredro* is personified most often by Juan, and this is justified, for Juan is he who advances the story. He summarizes the essential elements of the plot before the plot unfolds. In consequence of this function, he is the primary narrator of something which can neither be called frame-story, nor prologue or epilogue to the story proper. It is all of these and none of these, a mysterious centre, precedent and consequence, the cause and effect of the discourse. If we throw into relief the causal quality of the discourse on the first forty-one pages we find evidence of additional identification, more significant perhaps than the *paredro*, and certainly more obvious, between author-narrator and character-narrator.

This naturally raises the question of whether the secondary level narrators of the story in the strictest

sense of the word — whom Juan joins when he relates his
own part of the story — are not the extensions of the
primary level narrator, duplicates of the author-narrator. We shall attempt to corroborate this supposition in
other connections further on.

3) Kernel story, story lines

Before examining the lines of the story, we must find
a definition for the first forty-one pages. We believe
that "kernel story" is the most appropriate term due to
the double meaning of the word. It is from the kernel
that life commences, develops, and the kernel, the core
of everything, every thought, is equal to its essence.

Beyond the kernel story, the narrative runs on several lines. The story may be divided up according to location into Parisian, Viennese and London lines. This
horizontal classification is, however, rather approxima-
tive. As we shall see, the threads are mostly arranged
around conflicts originating in certain human relationships.

If we attempt to align the events in chronological
order, which is by no means unequivocal, we find that
the novel can be unravelled into sequences of events
that occur in the space of twenty-four hours, and all
other information concerning periods outside or beyond
these is brought into the narrative only in the form of
recollection, formally and essentially as an intercalated section of a sequence of events.

The events occurring in the three capitals can be
grouped around certain emotional nuclei: in London this
is Marrast's despairing love and Nicole's anguish at

being unable to return it, at the same time loving Juan
in the same hopeless way; in Paris it is Helène's despair
over the young boy who died on the operating table, and
in Vienna it is Juan's unreciprocated love for Helène.

This does not mean, however, that the action relates
directly to these emotional conflicts. In every case
those concerned seek solace in substitute activities:
Marrast collects a crowd of Neurotics Anonymous before
an insignificant painting in the museum and puts the
director of the museum in such a state that he has the
painting taken off the wall for fear of burglary; Juan,
in the company of Tell, shadows an elderly woman named
Frau Marta, who offers cheap lodgings to an English girl
and whose intentions they believe are not above suspi-
cion; Helène hopes to obliterate the death of her young
patient through the youth and vitality of Celia.

In London, the events of two days are recounted,
starting from morning till night. First day: Marrast
meets Calac and Polanco, and they get lost in the underground. In the meanwhile, Calac and Polanco discuss
swallows, Marrast converses about the purchase of a
block of stone with Whitlow, and tells him of his sus-
picion that one of the paintings in the museum whose
director, Harold Haroldson, is a distant relative of
Whitlow's wife, is in danger of being stolen. He returns
to the hotel to take Nicole to the museum, breaks the
wall of silence between them by his sincerity and by
doing so restores their relationship, if only for the
duration of their love-making. Second day: Marrast
leaves to arrange the transportation of the block of
stone to Arcueil; the *paredro* arrives in London, and Nicole phones to say that Tell has also arrived; Nicole
and Calac keep watch in the museum (Harold Haroldson has

172

the painting taken off the wall), then go on a binge
with Marrast. Nicole and Austin's leaving the restaurant
and spending the night together appears to be a continuation of this day. In fact the events of that night
occur a few days later.

If we divide the events of the two days in London
into two parts, the length of these correspond almost to
the last line: they are both thirty-three and a half
pages long. Of the subsequent happenings in London we
learn only through the conversation of those "shipwrecked" on the little island of the canal in the forest
of Vincennes.

Juan and his Danish girl-friend Tell arrive in
Vienna somewhat later than Marrast and the others to
London, and leave sooner, for it is to fetch Nicole that
Tell goes to London. Accordingly, the first part of the
London line is followed by the end of Juan's Christmas
Eve, but subsequently Juan and Tell's Viennese experi-
ences alternate with the events taking place in London
until the Parisian line appears just before the first
day ends in London.

In the Viennese line Juan describes the life he
lives there with Tell, the street and the house that
come to be associated with the motifs entangled in the
experience of the Christmas Eve, and returns to the re-
unions of the group in the café in Cluny, as well as to
the kernel story itself.

Following the informatory sections that give the
settings begins the Viennese thread, which lasts from
the night until the morning of the next day. The denouement of the Frau Marta episode is enigmatic. It is
quite possible that the girl is already dead when Juan
and Tell peep into the room from behind the door that

173

was left ajar. It is possible that the relationship between Frau Marta and the girl is Lesbian, but at the
same time the scene has an overtone of somnambulism. At
all events it becomes unreal when all the participants
of the scene leave the room through the door cut between
the two third-floor windows (which is absurd) and find
themselves in the City.

After these episodes — two in London, one in Vienna
and one in Paris with Celia and Helène — the events are
once more connected to three locations. The scene taking
place in the forest of Vincennes affords a comical frame
for a whole sequence of recollections, and this relieves
the strong emotional tension of the previous sections.
Paris follows Vincennes: the Juan-Helène episode, and
later the first night that Celia end Austin spend together. Both episodes begin in the afternoon.

The dawn that breaks after Juan and Helène's night
together is the dawn of the unveiling of Marrast's
statue, and the subsequent train-journey. All the members of the group are travelling on the train except
Marrast, who remained in Arcueil for the banquet following the unveiling of the statue. On the train the customary games of the group — the gobbledegook of Calas
and Polanco, their bets on the time Osvaldo the snail
will make in the race — alternate with thoughts, actual
events, wanderings in the City.

Helène reaches the City and the ever-sought hotel
room, where, upon her words of "Here I am", Austin's
knife plunges into her breast. Juan discovers the dead
Helène in the City, then makes for the canal where Nicole
stretches her arms out towards him. Frau Marta appears
and takes Nicole with her. In the closing section Polanco, Calac, the *paredro* and Tell overtake the train in a

taxi, and get Feuille Morte, left alone on it, to de-
scend. They surround Feuille Morte and the novel ends
with her words: bisbis.

3) The events: chronological order and place in the
   narration

The episodes that run parallel to each other do not
occur simultaneously even if there is only a few days'
difference between them. The sequence of the narrative
does not follow the chronological order of the individual episodes. The points of time and thus time itself
is not a factor to be reckoned with — what is more, is
negligible to the extent that the novel would not be
modified even if years were to pass between two events.
The sequence of events can only be followed within one
line of the story; it is impossible to establish any
sort of order relative to the whole of the narrative.
Let us take an example that will clearly illustrate that
two chains of events are impossible to collate chronolog-
ically. Tell arrives in London on the same day as the
paredro, though this is the day when Marrast is arranging the transportation of the block of stone; in other
words, he has not yet written the letter to Tell in
which he relates that Nicole has been unfaithful to him
with Austin, and it is because of this letter that Tell
goes to London to see Nicole. As for the other members
of the group, the *paredro* arriving in London at the same
time as Tell could only be Juan, but he has flown directly to Paris from Vienna to meet Helène, and is in any
case still in Vienna when Tell is already in London.

Considering the whole of the novel, therefore, the narrative is determined not by the chronological order of events, but by the similar motifs of the various lines; the discourse is, therefore, based upon accidental concurrences.

4) Frequency

The frequency deriving from repetition must necessarily be high in a work that entrusts the discourse to the concurrence of the various elements of the plot, that is, to repetition.

One of the sources of the high rate of recurrence is the repetition of an identical situation or relation: he/she who loves me I do not love, he/she whom I love does not love me (see the relation of Marrast-Nicole-Juan, or Nicole-Juan-Helène).

Nicole's relationship with Marrast ends with the night she spends with Austin. The Austin-Celia affair — which is a mirror-image, not a reproduction of this — is aimed at ending the Celia-Helène relationship. In both cases the outcome is doubtful, to say the least.

The episodes end upon a similar note almost without exception, which in itself assures a high frequency. Marrast and Nicole make love at the end of the first day in London, and it would not be unjustified to say that the second day ends the same way if we accept that the author merges the night on which Nicole and Austin make love with the night of the second day. In the three Parisian episodes it is Helène and Celia, Helène and Juan and Celia and Austin who make love, as do Juan and Tell in Vienna. Of this last we cannot say that the episode ends a coherent chain of events, therefore its value in the narrative cannot be compared to that of the previously listed instances.

With the exception of Vincennes and Arcueil, where the author does not focus the attention on the relationships between the members of the group, the sequences of events are all connected to the evening or the night. The days in London last from morning till night, those in Paris from the afternoon till the morning, and those in Vienna from the evening until morning. As we have seen, the factual inconsistencies invalidate calendar time, but the hour of the day is in itself a significant bearer of meaning. We shall attempt to interpret this meaning further on.

The alternation of the sequences of events connected to the three cities necessarily takes us back to the same locations again and again. Besides the repetition of the cities as scenes we may list the underground and the tunnel-like aspect of its corridors (in Paris it is in the Metro that Helène discovers the tunnel-like depth of the little girl's eyes on the Babybel poster; in London it is the two Argentines who lose their way in the maze of the underground), the hotel rooms (in London, in Vienna, and in the City), the trains (going to Calais, to Paris from Arcueil, departing from London), the restaurants (the Polidor in Paris, the restaurant of the Capricornio Hotel in Vienna, the London pub and the Marquee club), the red houses along the road leading from Venice to Mantua, mentioned repeatedly, the channels and canals (the Saint Martin, La Manche, and the canal in the forest of Vincennes), the meeting-place of the group: the café Cluny, the clinic, the Blutgasse in Vienna, mentioned several times, and the house with the

basilisk. To these are added the street with the high
pavements, the square of the trams, the arcades, the
corridors and rooms of the hotel, the lifts, the pontoons
and above all the trams themselves, all to be found in
the City. Every location in the City recurs repeatedly,
so it is obvious that the frequency of the narrative is
the highest when the characters "step into it".

A similarly high frequency is assured by the objects
and persons that surface in Juan's consciousness all at
once in the Polidor restaurant: the Sylvaner wine, Erzsébet Báthory, Frau Marta, the bloody castle, the Blutgasse, the basilisk (on Helène's brooch, on the house in
Vienna, on Monsieur Ochs's silver ring), the dolls, the
Butor book on Chateaubriand, the Chateaubriand steak.
All these appear in the poem intercalated in the kernel
story as well. Because of this, repetition is given, as
it were, but these elements are multiplied by the story
itself as they are by Juan's meditations in the Viennese
night.

The frequency of the narration is further augmented
by the repeated mention of certain parts of the body:
the eyes, the neck (throat), and the hand (fingers). The
English girl's eyes are "open, staring" (24) (p. 180),
Celia's are drooping, Helène's wide-open from insomnia;
Celia's, awakening to Helène's caresses, opening and
closing, awakening the next morning, stubbornly closed —
this is how she wants to persuade herself that all that
happened in the night was only a dream, but

> ... in her opened or closed eyes there was the same
> obstinate image before or after it was the same
> smell, cold and acid now, the same dirty fatigue...
> (25)

After the affair with Austin Marrast gives Nicole a
sleeping pill and

> She looked at me in a way that tried to say that, a
> kind of inconceivable thanks before dying... (26)

The episode of Frau Marta and the English girl, of Helène and Celia are connected by the motif that occurs in
both — the motif of the neck or throat: Helène caresses
Celia's throat, Frau Marta fiddles with the collar of
the English girl's pyjamas and the two purple dots are
supposedly put there by her vampire teeth (pp. 185, 187).

We know that Cortázar does not trust in the communicative power of the word. Instead of words that distort
true feelings and thoughts, he resorts to "body language". It is into the *hand*, embracing the most extensive field of contact, that he condenses the tending toward each other, the reaching out for each other that his
characters are unable or unwilling to express. The ungraspable, inconceivable experience of the Polidor restaurant makes Juan cry out

> You've got to leave something in my hands... (27)

The deepest desire, the most urgent necessity demands
immediate possession, realized through the body — the
hand — be it directed at the essence of existence or at
the beloved. The state of mind, the relation to the
other is reflected in many ways by the gestures of the
hand. Juan says of Nicole

> ... poor thing ... follows my shadow with her hands
> clasped...

Clasped hands are the sign of adoration, of mute appeal,
but at the same time of self-enclosed passivity. Nicole
knows that she would reach out for Juan in vain.

The hand of sleeping Nicole spreads out on the pillow
like a fern. This so very passive hand moves in sleep,
reaches for something in its unconsciousness, for something

which it knows to be unattainable. To Calac, who is in love with her, she tends a limp, languid hand which

... had slept in his hand for a moment. (29)

Marrast gives voice to his despair for not having his love requited by Nicole.

That isn't true not her hands only my hands (30)

The hand symbolizes sexual intercourse:

The hand you've let come to my pillow (31)

says Helène to the sleeping Celia. Celia's hand is innocent, a symbol of a natural rapprochement, natural life, the hope of Helène's redemption, while Helène's hand, "full of salt" (p. 278), is the symbol of a barren, withered life. Celia feels Helène's fingers stiffening on her throat. Her caresses are ominous, like Frau Marta's hands on the English girl's throat.

Juan says of himself

My sensitivity to hands is unhealthy (32)

The nameless reference in the kernel story

... as a hand slowly searches for the shape of a throat (33)

creates a connection between the hands of Frau Marta and Helène.

Of his unrequited love for Helène, Juan says

... it was still ... the distance of anguish to be almost touching you with my hands and seeing you get off at a corner and not being able to reach you, arriving too late once more... (34)

As she gives herself to Juan, Helène thinks

... he must have imagined ... his hands were looking for me again ... that finally I would get to the last meeting (35)

After the night that they spend together, Juan sits on the bank of the canal and

> ... once or twice he ran his *hand* across his *throat*
> as if it hurt a little. (*36*)

The sentence that succeeds this can only be interpreted
if we recognize the hidden similarities between Erzsébet
Báthory, Frau Marta and Helène

> If he'd had a pocket mirror he would have looked at
> his throat. It almost made him laugh that it was
> preferable not to have one alongside the dirty and
> black waters of the canal. (*37*)

In other words, he believes that Helène's shutting him
out of her love forever may have left a mark upon him,
and that if he saw this mark materialized, he would be
obliged to commit suicide. Finally, knowing that Helène
will never be his, he says to Tell

> Eyes are the only hands some of us have left... (*38*)

In the kernel story, Juan ponders

> I'll think to the very end that I might have been
> wrong ... that you yourself never understood what
> was going on, Helène ... that you simply played your
> cards badly ... And if I kept quiet, I would be com-
> mitting an act of betrayal ... and being silent would
> then be base. You and I know too much about something
> that isn't us and it locates these cards in which
> we're spades and hearts but not the hands that
> shuffle and deal them... (*39*)

This thought is repeated by Marrast, concerning the patterns of the kaleidoscope

> ... nobody could be and take away at the same time a
> little blue sliver or a purple bead, if he shook the
> tube and the figure formed all by itself, no longer
> able to be hand and figure at the same time. (*40*)

Even if we begin to deal the cards ourselves, the hand
that holds them is fate. The characters of the novel

accept a "fresh deal" — at times in the frame of such absurd games as putting an electric razor under power into oatmeal — but they have no power to rearrange life.

5) Modes of narration

The various modes of narration are not sharply distinguished in the novel. There is a relatively limited number of dialogues in which, despite the leisured narrative, a high frequency is ensured — not by the content, but by repeated constructions, phrases, or even entire sentences, as in the gobbledegook of Calac and Polanco.

In the City episodes, where the frequency is much higher, the mode of narration is most often of the summarizing type, being in fact interior monologue.

The pace of the interior monologue is not easily ascertainable. Since thinking is incomparably more rapid than speech, it seems particularly slow. The interior monologues relating to the City may, however, be conceived as factually experienced, lengthy, though not particularly eventful experiences. Approaching the question from this aspect these monologues are short and remarkably concise considering their content — in other words, they are in fact remarkably fast narratives.

These opposing aspects make the examination of the speed of the narrative unreal in a novel in which time itself is unreal, in which the subject of the narrative is not so much experience as the projection of that experience. If we consider not the events but their reflection in the consciousness, we naturally cannot speak of exact time. Even the gauging of the duration of the dialogues is made uncertain due to the fact that the author

embeds them into interior monologues. This interior monologue aspect is questionable, but the fact that it re-
cords interior action and that the narrator has no listener is a point in its favour.

Consequently, it is we, the readers, who are the
addressees, the narrataires of the interior monologues of
even the secondary level narrators. According to Genette,
the reader can only be the addressee, the audience of
the author. If we reverse this, the consequence of our
being the addressees is that the author must necessarily
be the narrator.

On this basis we can state that though Cortázar uses
all three modes of narration in *62...* (direct, indirect,
summarizing), he subordinates them to the interior monologue to such an extent that they are deprived of the
particular pace proper to them.

The comical dialogues, the longest of which is the
one conducted by the "shipwrecked" and those who hasten
to their aid in the forest of Vincennes may seem an exception. In the course of this conversation, the characters recall the events that occurred in London — now
in thought, now out loud. In both cases the narration is
indirect, its speed is therefore not easily ascertainable. And as far as the summary of the events then
taking place is concerned, it is questionable whether
the humorous rendering does not by necessity differ from
non-comical summaries, for it enters into minute details,
enrichening-transforming the factual description of
events with *fioritura*, as it were.

A natural consequence of humour is the upsetting of
proportions, the emphasis of insignificant elements to
the detriment or even disregard of the significant ones.
Humour in any case places its subject on an unreal level.

And on the level of unreality, the duration of the action must by necessity be unreal also. It therefore becomes clear that even the narrative speed of these episodes, taking place in the most real (or seemingly most real) surroundings, cannot be measured. Subsequently, it cannot be compared with the high frequency valid for the whole of the novel. (In the aforementioned episode, for example, the humourous effect is heightened by the repetition of the description of the inspector from London — a thin, black-suited individual holding an umbrella.)

6) Duration of the action and of the narration

In consequence of the contradictory sequence of events of the various story threads, the duration of the action is not only fictitious but unreal. If by action we mean the events or plot, situation, behaviour, sentiment and sensation appearing in the subjective consciousness, then a fairly long duration of narration accompanies an exceptionally short duration of action. The time intended for narration and the time measurable by the number of pages is equally distributed between the three plus one lines of the story (61 pages for each). The specification of three plus one can be made thanks to the fact that the number of main story threads is three (each of which abuts in a dénouement, albeit a negative one), while the plus one comprises the climate or atmosphere surrounding the group and characterized in the following quotation

> What had brought us together in the City, in the
> zone, in life, was precisely a merry and stubborn
> trampling of the Decalogues. The past had taught

each of us in his own way the profound uselessness
of being serious, of calling upon seriousness in
moments of crisis, of grasping its lapels and demand-
ing behaviours or decisions or renounciations; nothing could have been more logical than the tacit
complicity that had brought us together around my
paredros in order to understand existence and feelings in another way, to follow routes that were not
the ones advised in every circumstance... (*41*)

The sixty-one pages, besides giving a general account
of the situation, contain two sequences of events lasting from morning till night in Marrast's case; an account
of the situation and two sequences of events lasting from
late afternoon until morning in Juan's story, and two
sequences in Helène's. (The section dealing with the
night Juan and Helène spend together was naturally taken
into consideration in both story lines.)

The two great communal gatherings of the group (in
the forest of Vincennes, in Arcueil, and the train journey to Paris) begin in the afternoon. Only the second
ends late at night. Presumably Celia and Austin's tryst
takes place during this same period. It is in the night
that Marrast and Nicole, Juan and Helène part company
for ever. The kernel story begins and ends the story
proper on Christmas Eve, though these words lack validity
in the novel that is not cognizant of what went before
or after. Every story line issues from it and meanders
back into it. The City itself is nocturnal; this is the
reason why Juan would not have imagined that Tell could
also visit it, diurnal being that she is. Referring back
to Bataille, it is in the darkness of the spirit that we
can step outside ourselves and it is here that the il-
luminating moment of ecstasy can reach us. Juan, too,

hopes for enlightenment that may clear up the mystery of
fortuitous concurrences. It is, therefore, understandable that the night, too, holds a distinguished place in
the novel. In the symbolics of night and day, the former
is the domain of intimacy, of menace, of the search for
protection and companions, of looking for and of losing
the way, of mystery, and of the unveiling of mystery.
The lovers suffering from unrequited love, the struggles
and attempts of Helène incapable of love make tangible,
concrete in a way the conflict of existence of which
loneliness is only a projection. In final analysis, the
conflict of existence derives from the insolvable mystery
suggested by the concurrences, the unfathomable, mysterious nature of fate.

7) Levels of narrative - narrators and "narrataires"

A grading of these levels is questionable from the
outset in a novel in which "before" and "after" are non-
existent categories. The novel can be divided into a
kernel story and several story lines, but the narration
itself is a constant stream, an ebb and flow. It would
therefore be meaningless to qualify Juan first as a
primary level, then as a secondary level narrator. The
paredro, as we have already pointed out, attests to the
existence of a collective narrator.

8) Focalization

The narrative is consistently focalized from within,
as it were, since even the humourous rendering of events

is the result of the inner analysis, the internal interpretation of the individual characters. This exclusively
internal focalization — given that in any section of our
choice every member of the group becomes a narrator and
that in the personage of the *paredro* the group addresses
a listener who does not exist on the level of the story
as a collective narrator — points to the fact that the
vision inferred from the inner focalization multiplied,
enrichened by the nine narrators serves the also inter-
nally focalized discourse of the author. The narration
simply characterizes the speech of the author to the
reader, who is the only listener. (The individual narrators have apparent listeners only in the dialogues
intercalated into the summarizing monologues as parts of
the action that are the subject of their narration.)

9) Distance between narrator and story

The story, that is the subject of the narration is
not a mesh of objective acts, situations, behaviour etc.,
but the manifestation of all these in the subject, as is
ovident from the consistently inner focalization. This
is the reason why the summarizing-monologue type of narration affords maximal information, in other words, signifies minimal distance between the narrator and the
subject of his narrative.

There is no such minimal distance between the author
and his discourse, for this is not directed at facts
even to the extent that his narrators' discourses are.
In consequence of this, a peculiar situation develops:
while the narrators give maximal information in accordance with their interior monologues, the author — who is

multiplied in them as it were — does no more than attempt to produce the information he himself requires
with the aid of his discourse, and to approach thus the
mystery represented by the fortuitous concurrences attributed nevertheless to fate.

10) *The instant that triggers the narration*

The moment that launches the narrative, though it
cannot be denoted by any specific date, can definitely
be connected to the Christmas Eve in the Polidor restaurant. This exceptional concreteness of the moment
eliciting the narration (there can be no contradiction
concerning Christmas Eve) and its relatively dispropor-
tionate length compared to the story itself (nearly
forty pages) is due to the fact that it encodes the moment intitiating the discourse, in other words, the situation of conflict, the torturous presence of which is
the most significant reality for Cortázar.

11) *Narratorial presence*

The narrator–protagonists are naturally present in
the narrative. The protagonist-narrator Juan is also
present in the moment that launches the narrative. The
intercalated poem testifies to the presence of the
author, since in a nonepic poem the poet cannot be present fictitiously, as the poem itself is not fiction.

12) The symbolic quality of the narration

With the intercalated poem, the discourse gives final (though, as we have seen, not exclusive) proof of the symbolic quality of the narrative. It definitely points to the author as the composer of the poem. Cortázar does not portray the world, but himself, turning the attention of the reader to the questions that torment him in the firm belief that the conflict that tortures his being is equally torturous for the whole of mankind.

x x x

The application of the Genette-type examination of discourse to this narrative, of symbolic — what is more, lyrical-symbolic — value often yields negative results that differ from the likely variational possibilities. We have seen that it is as nonsensical to speak of primary and secondary level protagonist-narrators as it is to speak of various narrative levels. Any attempts to determine the factual-chronological order of the story lines is doomed to fail because of the contradictory references. The duration of the narration changes according to whether it is the action or event, or the subjective content of the consciousness that is considered its object. The three modes of narration lose their significance in the narrative that in the last analysis proves to be an interior monologue, and we can find no relation between these modes and the frequency of the narrative. No conclusion can be drawn from the provable presence of the protagonist-narrators, for they are simply multiplications or duplicates of the latently present author. These negatives convince us that this novel goes beyond

the bounds of its genre, verging on personal lyricism,
in which place is found — in overwhelming proportions,
what is more — for a treasure of motifs that ensure a
consistently high frequency.

This high frequency emphasizes the significance of
repetition. Three, or more than two represents the demand
for many variants in this work. The experimenting with
these variants awakens the hope that the author may at
least come close to the mystery of human existence even
if he is unable to solve it. It is perhaps sufficient to
refer to the three cities, the narrator-protagonists
— nine altogether —, and the obvious possibility of
arranging them into groups of three: Marrast-Nicole-Juan,
Juan-Helène-Celia, Nicole-Juan-Helène, and the three
levels of the action: the real, the imagined (Frau Marta)
and the ecstatic (the City). These three levels are
identical with the three phases of the author's existential conflict. In the real he discovers the mystery
manifest in fortuitous concurrences; in the imagined he
attempts to catch the hand responsible for these: fate or
the inevitable rules that govern it "in the act" as it
were (this is why he keeps watch on Frau Marta); and in
the ecstatic he approaches the brink of the possible by
almost losing himself, by almost reaching the other,
(as in the case of Juan-Helène), or reaches the brink of
the possible in death (as did Helène).

The members of the group can wander in the same ra-
tionally non-existent City because they represent the
author collectively — the author who objectifies his
lyrical self-conflict in his discourse.

The associative narrative based on the relation between the kernel story and the story lines is a discourse
that is in accordance with the syntax of Bataille's

philosophy. Bataille's opinion of language is reflected
in Cortázar's distrust of language and in the endeavour
to encode the forms or modes of human communication into
the language of gestures (hands). Night is given preference over the other parts of the day, for in Bataille's
philosophy night is the most suitable interval for the
losing and the enlightenment of the self. The various
story lines make possible the theoretical trying out of
behaviour patterns in identical situations of conflict.
Consequently, the narrative is symbolic in quality: the
encoding of the meditation over the conflict of the self.

Notes

*The philosophy of Bataille and the world image of Julio
Cortázar*

(*1*) Georges BATAILLE: *Oeuvres Complètes. V. La Somme
    athéologique. 1. L'expérienece intérieure.* Galli-
    mard, Paris, 1973.
(*2*) Julio CORTAZAR: *62: A Model Kit.* (62. Modelo para
    armar). Random House, New York, 1972, 249.
(*3*) ibid. 6.
(*4*) ibid. 7.
(*5*) ibid. 28.
(*6*) BATAILLE, op. cit. 38.
(*7*) ibid. 231.
(*8*) CORTAZAR, op. cit. 104.
(*9*) BATAILLE, op. cit. 57.
(*10*) BATAILLE, op. cit. 67.
(*11*) CORTAZAR, op. cit. 105.
(*12*) ibid. 105.
(*13*) BATAILLE, np. cit. 343.
(*14*) CORTAZAR, np. cit. 98.
(*15*) BATAILLE, op. cit. 176.
(*16*) CORTAZAR, oŭ. cit. 177.
(*17*) ibid. 177-168.
(*18*) ibid. 93.
(*19*) ibid. 93.
(*20*) ibid. 94.
(*21*) ibid. 65.
(*22*) BATAILLE, op. cit. 142.
(*23*) CORTAZAR, op, cit. 104.

(24) ibid. 180.
(25) ibid. 191.
(26) ibid. 193.
(27) ibid. 10.
(28) ibid. 37.
(29) ibid. 213.
(30) ibid. 204.
(31) ibid. 182.
(32) ibid. 80.
(33) ibid. 13.
(34) ibid. 227.
(35) ibid. 268.
(36) ibid. 275.
(37) ibid. 275.
(38) ibid. 259.
(39) ibid. 36-37.
(40) ibid. 49.
(41) ibid. 85.

VI. SUMMARY

If there is no narrator and if the story, the sum
total of the sequence of events is told by the author,
then narrative and discourse to all intents and purposes
coincide. If, however, the novel has a protagonist-narrator or several narrators, the author's discourse is
directed at the organization of the narrative or rather
at the sum total of narrations and their relation to
each other. In such cases, the story proper contains the
signs (climate, character, symbols, mythical motifs,
events or elements of action) that constitute a system
in the narration. It is into this system that the author
encodes his world image, drawn from his experiences, in
accordance with his ideological or philosophical training. The narrative replaces the action when the portrayal
of reality makes way for the portrayal of the author's
world image.

In the works analysed, the discourse organizes not
the action, but the narrative (considering the dual nature of *One Hundred Years of Solitude*: on the one hand
the absence of a protagonist-narrator, the action-
centredness of the novel, on the other hand, the story
already written on the parchments of Melquíades as an

exception and at the same time a confirmation). The narrative is launched by a nostalgic (Rulfo, Onetti, García Márquez) or a meditative (Vargas Llosa, Cortázar) moment. It is worthy of note that the method of the two novels evolving from a meditative moment were most effectively exposed through the analysis of their discourse, despite the fact that, of all the works here analysed, it is these that represent most markedly the two extremes: the realistic description of society and internal action, taking place at least in part in the irrational. There is a sharp contrast between the eminently social-ideological viewpoint of Vargas Llosa, and the philosophy of Bataille, which is as far removed from sociality as possible, but which unquestionably permeates Julio Cortázar's *62....*

Besides direct and indirect speech, one of the most frequently and generally used modes of narration is the interior monologue, a peculiar form of summary. In accordance with these modes, the speed of the narration is relatively slow. (If we consider only its mode of narration, *One Hundred Years of Solitude* differs from the other novels in that it is largely made up of summaries which cannot be qualified as interior monologues.)

The gauging of the relation between the speed of the narration and the duration of the action is hampered, made doubtful in every work discussed by time made unreal in some way or another. (From this point of view the speed of *One Hundred Years of Solitude* is questionable also.)

The narration, generally qualifiable as leisured or slow, is accompanied by a high frequency. This may in itself slow down the procession of the narrative, for it repeats certain relations or connections already apparent

194

in it. Many elements in these novels increase the frequency in so consistent a manner that an impression of a circle closing in upon itself is created in the reader. The discourse utilizing the system of feedbacks, the chronology and the contradictory order of events established in the narration all serve to demonstrate timelessness, time repeated cyclically, spinning vortex-like or imprisoned labyrinth-fashion. Every type contradicts the historicity of time. The attack upon time stands for the rejection of the given society in the case of Rulfo, García Márquez and Vargas Llosa, and to a certain extent in the case of Onetti as well, though he — like Cortázar — accuses human condition above all else. The incapability of man to create and establish contact, communication, is the concern — though not the sole concern — of the first three writers as well.

The predominantly interior monologue type of narration, like the dialogues and the summaries describing the perceptible, shorten the distance between the narrator and the action in almost every case, for each gives precise and detailed information. In dialogues, the narrator disappears — unless the author makes an observation from which it becomes clear which of the speakers is the narrator. This type of dialogue, like the interior monologue, ensures maximal information in addition to the presence of the narrator. In these novels the narration only appears to be continuous; in effect, only an infinitesimal part of the virtually complete sequence of events is presented, but the informative value of the narrated parts is remarkably high.

In this respect also *One Hundred Years of Solitude* makes use of a singular device. It interfuses the impersonal, absent, narrator and the remarkably fast summary

of events with the aid of comments that betray the unexpressed presence of the narrator, and by doing so
shorten the distance between the narrator and the action — for in these highly informative commentaries he
reveals the sentiments of the characters, describes certain scenes in exceedingly fine detail and forms an opinion of the given situation. The duality of this procedure
connects him with the other characters, but at the same
time sets him apart from them. He pairs minimal information to his absence, maximal information to his concealed
presence. The distance between himself and the action
often changes from sentence to sentence. This sheds light
upon the focalization of the narrative: outer and inner
focuses follow each other without progressivity, though
the author never hands over his role of narrator.

Onetti proceeds in a similar fashion, though in his
case inner focalization is less frequent, as is the presence of the author-narrator that accompanies it. Many
protagonist-narrators of *The Shipyard* and of *Pedro Páramo*, like those of *Conversation in the Cathedral* and
62..., are most often, though not necessarily present in
their own narratives. The outer or inner focalization of
these narratives depends on the place they occupy within
the story, and on the interests or personality of the
narrator.

The alternation of outer and inner focuses thus
characterizes every work analysed, though the rate of
alternation never attains the frequency of *One Hundred
Years of Solitude*. The reason for this — besides the absence of a protagonist-narrator — must be sought in the
author's intenion to counterbalance the rapid summary
that conveys minimal information and keeps a distance
between the author-narrator and the action.

In the sequence of events of any novel there comes a moment when a hiatus becomes necessary. It is indisputable that in modern epics the frequency with which this happens either far exceeds the desired measure or certain episodes are described in excessive detail (both may occur within the same novel). The sequence of events of the works analysed are generally incomplete, greatly fragmented. These hiatuses are covered up partly by the unascertainable and contradictory duration of time, partly by the minutely described episodes. The intimated, but neither expounded, nor motivated, thoughts, gestures, in many cases the comments themselves — which do not derive directly from what they relate to — all attest to an elliptic discourse. The symbolics of these hiatuses, relating to the fragmentary quality of the world image, are self-evident.

From a solely esthetic point of view, the ellipse is one of the most characteristic figures of poetry, and as such contributes greatly to the shift of Latin American novels towards poetry. Naturally, the symbolic motifs, the thermal and sound environment, which may be thought of as belonging to the realm of scenics, and the repetition of the most diverse elements all call to mind the devices of poetry. The fact that the narrative is the encoding of the author's world image in itself signifies a giant step from epics towards poetry, given that the narrative elements are as connotative as the elements of poetry. It would not be easy to classify the works under discussion according to their degree of poeticalness. For example, *Conversation in the Cathedral*, the most "prosaic" of all the novels in its linguistic idiom as we have seen, builds its discourse upon association to an exceptionally high degree. In *62...* it is association that determines the order of the various story lines. The discourse of *62...* even converts to a regular, genuine poem, yet we feel that Rulfo's language, his mode of construction — which can hardly be qualified as prosaic — is more suggestive — more poetic. It is the close unity of the objective and the poetically intuitive that charms us in *The Shipyard* as in *One Hundred Years of Solitude*.

By way of illustration, allow me to quote a single passage from this last novel

After that for over ten days they did not see the sun. The soil became soggy and wet like the ashes from a volcano, the vegetation grew rank and treacherous, the screeching of the birds and the shrieking of the monkey sounded from further and further afield and *the world became everlastingly sad.* This dampness, this silence, this paradise as yet unaware of original sin, where boots sank deep into steaming oily puddles, where knives sliced lilies that bled crimson and salamanders that glistened gold into two awoke age-old memories in the members of the expedition. They stumbled along like sleepwalkers for a week, hardly uttering a word in this sad jungle, in the dim light cast by hordes of phosphorescent insects, their lungs heavy with the stifling smell of blood. (*1*)

Every author, even Vargas Llosa, who is particularly wont to individualize his characters, searches for what is common in their personages. This aim is expressed in the multiplication of personalities and proves in final analysis that the author is interested not in the faculties or individual features but in the answer of his personae to the given challenge. This singular character formation tends from the Vargas Llosa type of triplication of personalities to the collective character, who is by nature particularly apt to convey the author's world image — not through his words, but through his behaviour.

The experience determining the world image of the author — challenge and answer to the challenge — is concentrated to such an extent in the collective character functioning as narrator that the identification of narrator and author (as in *62...*) is virtually inevitable.

García Márquez is the only one who consistently remains true to the traditional third person narrative, which can in no way be assigned to a protagonist-narrator. The passage cited above enlightens his attitude of author-narrator. The author's manifestations, switching from outer focalization, of the visible, perceivable, to inner focalization concerned with sentiments and ideas, affect the reader with the same testimonial subjectivity as do the protagonist-narrators. In other words, what García Márquez does is to unite the impersonal and the subjective narrator. Essentially, all the authors strive to do the same, either by masking what is subjective and human with objectivity, or by presenting objective facts with strong subjective emphasis.

What readers in general expect from the novel is determined by the traditional realistic and naturalistic tendencies of the past century even today. Scholes and Kellog in their work entitled *The nature of the narrative* examined the changing characteristics of narrative works in the course of the history of epics and came to the conclusion that a narrative may be representational (and, within this category, either historic or mimetic) or illustrative (which also consists of two branches: the romantic novel or romance, destined to illustrate the truth of beauty, and the didactic, destined to illustrate the truth of thought). According to Scholes and Kellog, the illustrative novel does not reproduce actuality (actual, valid reality), but presents certain selected aspects of the actual, besides certain essences referable to ethical and metaphysical truths. (2)

If it is true that the novels discussed do not present the world but give only a possible model of it, thereby influencing the reader, forcing him to side with them, mobilizing him, then we must say that these works are the illustrations of their authors' thoughts about the world and as such are didactic in character. The romantic novel and the didactic narrative belong by nature to the category of fiction *par excellence* — the fictitious tale that has no pretensions of portraying reality, as opposed to the empiric, directly experimental, representational novel. Within the liberal bounds of fiction, there is place for mythical and unreal elements alike, for "conceptualized" characters, for illogical or irrational plots, for unreal space and time, for humour nourished by the absurd, for straying onto the territories of other genres. In all these is manifest the desire of the author to recapture his "innocence". (3)

At the same time, it is indisputable that the ideas they form of the world are not identical with their world image, for this last represents much more than is intellectually apprehensible: it stands for a complex, contradictory, emotionally charged, global experience. It is due to this that mimesis, (4) the eminently realistic reproduction of experienced reality, manifest formally also in interior monologue or dialogue, is frequent in all the novels.

Didactic intent is worthless if it is ineffective. The identification of the reader will take place all the more readily — or perhaps only — if he can recognize himself, his surroundings, society, community, or his own personal problems in the novel. The inextricable web of the fictitious and the empirical, the illustrative didactic and the representational reproductive covers every layer of our human condition in the works discussed. Even if these cannot encompass the entirety of the world, they do manage to find a way to the whole being of the reader, and thus do not leave unfulfilled his desire for completeness.

Two of our authors do not renounce the great ambition of the realistic novel: the representation of the historical-sociological aspect of the world. Both of them alloy the originally representational reproductive type of novel with eventful fiction. Almost all of these novels do this to some extent, but these go far beyond the ensurance of a good plot and plenty of action. Vargas Llosa is not content to search for a guiding principle or principles to direct his portrayal of the panorama of society, but turns to a peculiarly hair-raising type of entertainment: the detective story, and builds his novel around a mysterious murder.

García Márquez tends towards the historical and the sociological (in this he is realistic) and to the drawing of conclusions and moral lessons that are historical or sociological in tenor (in this he is didactic), and makes romantic fiction out of his work: his world is mythical and miraculous; in his romance it is rhetorics, a masterly use of language, that is destined to approach final truth. In other words, it is poetry and the myth that creates itself which captivates the reader, makes him accept the truth that García Márquez holds valid for society and in personal life alike.

In medieval didactic art, it was rhetorics (5) that ensured the pleasure which contributed to the understanding and acceptance of the moral, serving as a conveyor, like the essentially inimitable base or vehicle does in natural foods or herbs. The significance of rhetorics (in the positive sense of the word) is obvious from the poeticalness and the characteristic discourse of the works discussed.

As the characteristics of the ingredients of a chemical compound are modified when they come into contact with each other, creating a new quality, so the alloying of several types of novel initiates complex processes (6) in which action and world image, entering a relationship of interaction, modify one another, giving new meaning to the former, and the persuasive force of actuality to the latter.

According to Scholes and Kellog, there is a tendency in literature which began in the Middle Ages by rationalizing myth into allegory and tended to rationalize it as mimetic fiction, a trend coinciding with the development of European rationalism, which tends from the abstract intellectualizing of medieval thought towards the empiricism of modern science. (7)

On this basis we may say that in our novels' historical—mimetic representation is the illustration of the world image of the individual authors, didactic allegories in which empiricism appears on the level of intellectual abstraction.

From this, however, we may conclude that the tendency begun in medieval times and lasting to the present day has been — at least according to the testimony of these novels — reversed, and now tends from the representational-mimetic towards the illustrative-didactic. Naturally, we do not equate our present-day culture with that of the Middle Ages. But we cannot bypass the question of how far the tending towards ethical or metaphysical truth accompanying the didactic genre characterizes contemporary Latin American novels.

Ethical truth — or at least ethical truth in the traditional sense of the word — does not interest our authors. This is signalled by the fact that they attach no importance to the traits or endowments of their personages.

As far as metaphysical truth is concerned, metaphysical thinking and cognitive processes undoubtedly do characterize these novels, since they portray phenomena as *a priori* gives, unchanging, invariable, and the incidentally selected, discontinuous episodes of the narratives reflect a point of view that sees phenomena as independent of, or at least isolated from, one another.

All this, however, could relate to the creation of models only. This vehicle of contemporary science originates in the obstacles impeding cognition. In science and in experience reality is no longer formulated in the way it used to be. Every feature which goes beyond the former image of reality is *meta*physical, transcendental in the proper sense of the word — namely in that it transcends the limits of the familiar, the known.

The supernatural motifs of the novels under discussion are nourished by a double demand: by the demand to transcend irrational reality (the creating and mainte-

nance of senseless social and personal relationships) on
the one hand, reduced, fragmented reality that is no
longer congruent with the entirety of experience on the
other. (These supernatural motifs are by no means the
only devices used to make this "transcending" possible;
Vargas Llosa's discourse is "transcendental", and the
Onetti type play-acting goes far beyond what is tradi-
tionally meant by reality.)

The metaphysical and transcendental quality does not
arise from the desire to come to know reality existing
outside our world, but from the endeavour directed at
the constitution and cognizance of a reality appropriate
to our age, a reality that has at its disposal wider
limits than formerly.

It may be supposed that in a critical situation, when
"transcendental" cognizance appears to be indispensible,
the volition directed towards this cognizance is a prime
ethical necessity. The didactic intent of the novels discussed therefore relates to "metaphysical" and ethical
truth alike.

Notes

Summary

(1) GARCIA MARQUEZ: *One Hundred Years of Solitude.*
Harper and Row, New York, 1970. 11.

(2) "Illustration differs from representation in narrative art in that it does not seek to reproduce actuality but to present selected aspects of the actual, essences, referable for their meaning not to historical, psychological or sociological truth but to ethical and metaphysical truth."
Robert SCHOLES and Robert KELLOG: *The nature of narrative.* Oxford University Press. New York, 1966. 88.

(3) "Realism has proved so powerful an agent in narrative art that its influences may never wholly disappear; literary artists may never recapture totally the innocence of pre-novelistic romance." ibid. 85.

(4) "The connection between the fictional world and the real can be either representational or illustrative ... The illustrative is symbolic; the representational is mimetic." ibid. 84.

(5) "...while most medieval narrative is consciously didactic it is just as consciously rhetorical." ibid. 140.

(6) "... when ... purely emotional situations or events are combined with allegorical situations or events, the tension between ethical and esthetic impulses can become complex, working modifications in both story and meaning." ibid. 99.

(7) "... historical shift away rationalizing myth as allegory to rationalizing it as mimetic fiction, a shift which coincided with the development of European rationalism away from the abstract intellectualizing of medieval thought to the empiricism of modern science." ibid. 138.